Kauai
STORIES

The island of
KAUA'I

Hanalei Bay

Ke'e Beach

Ha'ena

Napali Coast

Hanakapi'ai

Hanakapi'ai

Kalalau Valley

Koke'e
State Park

Poli'hale
State Park

Waimea Canyon

Mt. Wai'ale'a
Wettest spot on eart

Nohili Point

Barking Sands
Pacific Missle
Range

Mana Point

Kekaha • Waimea

N

W   *E*

S

Kaumakani

Ele'ele   La

Salt Pond
Beach Park

Hanapepe

0 1 2 3 4 5 6   553 Sq. Miles

Lawa'

Princeville

Kilauea Lighthouse

ei Bay

Kilauea

Moloaa Bay

Anahola

'a'eale'e
on earth

Opaeka'a Falls

Kapa'a   Kealia

Wailua

Wailua Falls   Wailua River

Kilohana
Crater

Lydgate
State Park

Lihu'e

Nawiliwili Bay   Goodnight '15

Kalaheo

Koloa

awa i

Kipu Kai

Po'ipu

Maha'ulepu

Pacific
Ocean

Kauai

STORIES

PAMELA VARMA BROWN

BathrobePress.com
A division of Write Path LLC
Kapaa, Kauai, Hawaii

BathrobePress.com
A division of Write Path, LLC
Kapaa, Hawaii 96746

Cover: "Cottage #10" by Fanny Bilodeau
Cover design: Aaron Yadao, Ink Spot Printing, Kauai, Hawaii
Book interior production: Judah Freed, Hoku House, Kauai, Hawaii

First edition: September 2012
Second edition: May 2015

ISBN: 978-0-9856983-5-5 (Paperbook)
ISBN: 978-0-9856983-4-8 (ebook)

Library of Congress Control Number: 2012943485

To Lincoln, and to my family,
I love you with all my heart

To Michel

To all Kauai people

Acknowledgments

My heartfelt thanks to everyone who graciously opened their homes, phone lines and Skype connections to share your personal stories in interviews for this book, and to those of you who wrote your own stories. Every day you demonstrate the spirit of aloha that I have experienced since moving to Kauai more than 25 years ago. It is an honor and a privilege to share your stories with people who want to be inspired, entertained and to learn more about life on this Garden Island.

A million thank yous to Fanny Bilodeau for your beautiful painting on the cover of this book. Your artwork captures the warmth and spirit of Kauai, and your own story, told in this book, reminds us that dreams do come true when we follow our passion.

Mahalo (*thank you*) to Judah Freed for all your expertise, hours and care in bringing my vision of the interior of this book into reality.

Mahalo to the very talented Diane Goodnight for your beautiful hand-drawn map of Kauai.

Thank you to my friends who took the time and cared enough to proofread the manuscript for this book: Marta Lane, Scott Douglass, Karen McInnis, Denise Roberts and the champion editor, Andy Johnston. Huge mahalo to you all!

Lincoln, my eternal gratitude for your love, support, ideas, encouragement and sharing of my vision. I couldn't have done this without you — and wouldn't have wanted to.

And mahalo to Michel Vinet for allowing me to make a good living while pursuing my dreams.

With much aloha,

Pamela Varma Brown
August 2012 & March 2015

Note: The Hawaiian language employs a handful of diacritical marks, including an okina, that looks like an upside down apostrophe, to indicate proper pronunciation of Hawaiian words. For example, when the okina is used, Kauai is written as Kaua'i. Okinas and other Hawaiian diacritical marks have been intentionally omitted from this book to make easier reading for those who are unfamiliar with the Hawaiian language.

Please also note that in the Hawaiian language, plural forms of many words are the same as the singular. For example, the plural of lei is lei, rather than leis.

Contents

Working for the Plantations

Chicken Nuggets

Kauai & World War II

Kauai's Ocean

Music on Kauai

Hiking Kauai

Wayfinding

Kauai
STORIES

The Spirit of Kauai

The Setting

The island of Kauai is one of the most beautiful places in the world. It's the oldest of all the Hawaiian islands, created five million years ago by a volcano, Mount Waialeale, located in the center of the island.

After Mount Waialeale cooled, lava was ground to bits for eons by ocean waves. Ever so slowly, the 50 miles of white sand beaches that circle the island were formed. Kauai's mountainous regions were carved by wind, rain and waterfalls, into steep ridges and deep, lush valleys. Kauai is aptly nicknamed The Garden Island.

At only 550 square miles, Kauai is the smallest of the four most populated Hawaiian islands. It is quite isolated in the middle of the Pacific Ocean, nearly 2,500 miles from the continental United States to the east, and almost 4,000 miles from Japan to the west. As a result, people on the Garden Island tend to be independent, courageous and determined. They are also some of the kindest and most generous people on the planet.

More than half of Kauai's population of 65,000 people are descendents of immigrants who came from other countries to work in Hawaii's sugar plantations. Beginning in the mid-1800s, laborers came from the Philippines, Japan, China, Puerto Rico, Portugal, Korea, Spain and Germany. The last Kauai sugar plantation harvested its final crop in 2009, but the island is still a true melting pot of cultures.

Opaekaa Falls, on Kauai's eastern shore.
(Photo by Pamela Varma Brown)

Life on the Garden Island is relaxed, with a small-town friendliness everywhere you go. A visit to the grocery store often turns into an encounter with acquaintances, and with more than 1 million visitors annually, there are always opportunities to make new friends.

Kauai's stunning scenery often takes center stage, but those who live on Kauai know it's the spirit and warmth of the island's people that make Kauai one of the most special places in the world.

Hula

In its earliest forms, the hula was performed only by men, wearing brightly-colored leaves of ti plants, or nothing at all, in a powerful, almost primal dance. Over time, women joined in, and the dance was transformed into performances for pleasure, as we know it now.

In the 1820s, hula was almost lost entirely, when missionaries who arrived in Hawaii pushed heavily for the cultural dance to be prohibited. Hula was banned. One missionary society called it a "public evil."

For 50 years, Hawaiian culture went underground. The very few people who kept it alive, did so in relative secret.

In the 1870s, Hawaii's last king, David Kalakaua, began shepherding the re-emergence of Hawaiian culture, including hula, back into the public sphere. Kalakaua was known as "The Merrie Monarch" for his love of song, dance and parties, and he is the namesake for the world's most prestigious hula celebration, the Merrie Monarch Festival, that takes place annually on Hawaii Island.

Today, two forms of hula are performed by both men and women. The first is kahiko *(ancient)*, in which dancers wear ti leaf skirts or natural fabrics, flower or fern lei around their heads, and fern bracelets around their wrists and ankles. The second is auana, meaning to wander or drift, a beautiful, flowing modern hula often set to contemporary music, in which males wear long-sleeved blouses tucked into trousers and women wear long graceful dresses.

Keeping Hula Alive
Leinaala Pavao Jardin

Leinaala Pavao Jardin began dancing hula when she was three years old, continuing through high school and college, earning titles along the way including Miss Keiki (Child) Hula of Kauai, and winning the coveted Hawaiian Language Award at the Merrie Monarch Festival, the world's most prestigious hula celebration. Leinaala became a kumu (teacher) and started her own hula halau (school) on Kauai in 1997 named Halau Ka Lei Mokihana o Leinaala. Her students continue to win numerous titles.

Leinaala's dark eyes shine brightly as she speaks enthusiastically and joyfully about hula, laughing heartily and often, hands intuitively forming hula movements as she illustrates stories. She shares her journey to becoming a kumu, hula history on Kauai and the responsibility she feels for keeping Hawaii's traditional dance alive.

Hula Became Real

Hula is my passion. When I dance, I feel humbled but filled with pride. We are fortunate to be able to dance the hula because it was lost for so long.

I studied hula growing up on Kauai and that was my foundation, but when I went to the Big Island for college at the University of Hawaii at Hilo and joined Kumu Rae Fonseca's halau *(school),* that's when I really learned about hula. When he gave you your mele *(song)*, he didn't give you the English to it. It was in Hawaiian and you translated it together as a group, everybody dictionary in hand.

We learned how mele were composed. Normally if you're writing a song about a loved one, you don't even make mention of that

Leinaala Pavao Jardin dancing
hula auana as a nine-year-old.
(Photo courtesy Leinaala Pavao Jardin)

loved one. You compare that person to a special flower or a special bird. Composers use the blossom as a metaphor for a loved one or a relationship. If a song is about surfing, the surfboard going in and out of the waves could be a metaphor for making love. That's why when teaching hula, I've got to research the mele. I can't just pick a song and teach it. If it's a surfing song, I have no idea what's behind it, and here I'm going to send out 12 little boys dancing this song!

When I studied with Kumu Rae, we made all our implements; we made all our leis. When I had been with his halau for only about three or four months, there were probably about 100 ladies trying out for the Merrie Monarch Festival and I got selected! Rae said, "Everybody has to sew their dresses." So I called my mom and said, "You have to find me a seamstress." Little did I know that he meant that we were going to sew our *own* dresses. That is when hula became real to me. It wasn't store-bought.

How About You Start Teaching?

I studied under Rae for four years. When I graduated from college, I came home to Kauai to take care of my mom, Mary Ann Pavao, who was battling cancer at that time. I said, "Please, this can't be the end of hula for me." I called up my kumu and said, "I'm so torn. I want to dance but I want to take care of my mom."

He said, "How about you start teaching? Find the closest senior center. Ask if you can teach the kupuna *(grandparent's generation)*. That's where you start and you're going to learn from them, too." Guess where I live? Right next door to the senior center!

My first class was so much fun, but they taught me! I called my kumu and said, "This is not going well." He said, "That's why you start there, because they don't want someone younger teaching them because they're really the teachers." I took them to the Kupuna Hula Festival in Kona on the Big Island, it's like the Merrie Monarch for kupuna, and we won first place!

My kumu said, "I think you're ready to start your own halau (*school*). Hold a registration and see how many people show up."

On registration day, I was so nervous. I was inside the house and I asked my mom, who was sitting outside, "Is there anyone out there?" I thought there might be maybe two students. My mom said, "Uh, yeah, you may want to hurry and come out." I came out and the line was going all the way around the house! I've been teaching hula ever since then.

My kumu passed away unexpectedly when he was only 56 years old. He only uniki (*graduated*) six of us to become kumu in his lifetime. Usually it's a dozen or more. So when I dance and when I teach, it is to keep his name alive.

In hula, the genealogy is very important. My goal is when you see my students come out on stage, you can say, "that's Rae's girl." And because it's Rae's girl, it's Uncle George Naope's style, and Auntie Iolani Luahine's style. As much as I want to get creative, I've got to make sure that when I step up on that stage, that when my dancers dance, 30, 40 years from now, that people can say, "That came from Kumu Rae, that came from Uncle George, from Auntie Io." In the hula world, that's how it is done.

Feel the Mist

I want my students to feel love for our Hawaiian culture, love for the hula because you are sharing our culture, and to dance with the utmost respect for the composer who took the time to write that

Leinaala Pavao Jardin performing hula kahiko in the 1993
Merrie Monarch Festival Miss Aloha Hula Competition.
(Photo courtesy Leinaala Pavao Jardin)

mele. That song means a lot to the person who wrote it; you're delivering their story.

You have to put yourself in the location that the song is written about. If you're dancing about Kokee, you better feel the chill of that mountain climate when you're dancing so your audience can feel it.

When my niece, Jaedyn, was nine years old, I entered her in the Miss Keiki Hula competition. She was dancing to "Manowaiopuna," named after the waterfalls in Hanapepe Valley that were featured in the Jurassic Park movie. Jaedyn's grandparents used to live in that valley. I wanted her to see the falls, to feel the mist on her skin.

A week before the competition, we chartered a helicopter and landed there. Jaedyn danced at the base of the waterfall and we cried and we all got wet from the spray of the falls. The next week, she won Miss Keiki Hula.

Hula Started on Kauai

Hula is an important part of the Hawaiian culture. It was always much more than entertainment. It was the only form of communication for Hawaiians for centuries because we didn't have a written language until the early 1800s. It kept stories alive about Pele *(volcano goddess)* and other gods, about the different aumakua *(spiritual guardians)* and the genealogy of all our ancestors.

In ancient times, women were totally forbidden from doing the hula. It was done only by men who would do it to prepare for battle. It was the best, finest form of training that they knew. So a lot of the ancient hula, it's very vigorous, like if you put a spear in their hands they could hurt someone! Eventually the men started to go off to war and that is when the women took a liking to hula. I always joke that it's like everything in life: men started it, women learned how, we got better at it and we took over.

The beliefs and traditions of hula can slightly differ from halau to halau. What I share is what was taught to me. I believe that hula started on Kauai because we are the oldest island. A lot of songs are written about Kauai, so people on other islands are dancing to songs about our island!

In early years, hula was danced only to chanting, not to instrumental music. The first beat that hula was set to was to the pahu, a drum from Tahiti, traditionally made from the coconut tree with sharkskin as the head or cover. Records show that the first place the pahu arrived in Hawaii was on Kauai. When you study to become a kumu, you have to carve your own pahu. I carved my own; it stayed at my kumu's halau on the Big Island when I graduated. After my kumu passed on, I brought my pahu home to Kauai.

A song has verses and you do every verse twice. Most hulas used to be done with all movements beginning to the right, but Kauai hula teachers developed a style to create more balance. Now, the first verse you start moving to the right; the second time you start to the left. Everybody knows that style of hula originated on Kauai.

There are two types of hula: kahiko, the ancient, and auana, which is more modern and was developed after the missionaries arrived in Hawaii. Kahiko is very traditional; these are very old mele talking about the birth of the islands, gods and restating history.

Hula kahiko danced to the pahu is the most sacred form of hula. When you learn a hula pahu, the idea is to deliver it almost exactly as it was taught to you; there's no room for innovation. You shouldn't be smiling, it's somber, you stay very humble. The pahu is where the attention is placed, and not on the dancer.

As you move along time and history, there's more room for creativity, so if you're doing a kahiko mele about Queen Liliuokalani or King Kalaukaua, who are contemporary, you can put a smile in there.

It's hard for me to not smile, so I prefer to dance auana. But I prefer teaching the ancient kahiko. I love seeing what was taught to me, in front of me, to see it living on. To watch 40 or 50 of my women students do a traditional hula is very powerful.

Hula is in Your Heart: Teaching in Japan

I am now also teaching hula in Japan, picking up a relationship my kumu started when he trained a Japanese man's daughter to dance. When my kumu passed away, I said, "I'll go."

There are more hula dancers in Japan than there are in Hawaii. I have taught groups of 100 women but there are some kumu who go to Japan whose halau average 500 or 1,000 students. There are competitions and huge concerts there.

When my daughter, Breeze, the 2009 Miss Keiki Hula in Hawaii, was hired to dance in Japan, they had security for her. To them, Miss Keiki Hula is a big star. It was so funny: they ran up and were yelling "Kawaii! Kawaii!" I was thinking, "They really love our island." I found out later that kawaii means cute or precious in Japanese.

Some Hawaiians think in order to dance hula, you have to be on the aina *(land)* in Hawaii, so I never thought I would teach hula in Japan. But my belief now is, how do we perpetuate it? Why not go there and share?

Hawaiian culture has been extremely popular in Japan for a long time. I finally figured out why. Their culture is so serious. In their lifestyle, they're not allowed to show the kind of joy as we have in hula. They can't play, and in their traditional dances, the women don't smile. Hula is totally opposite; it's joyful. I teach my Japanese classes that hula is not about what you see in the mirror. It's about what you see inside, in your heart.

The Blessings Keep Coming

I'm probably known as one of the strictest hula teachers on Kauai. My students know I love them dearly and there is a time to have fun and play, but when it's hula time, we do tough training. Sometimes the kids and even my adult students, I see them teary-eyed and it breaks my heart. But I believe, as in anything in life, you have to work hard, you have to be committed.

When we enter the Keiki Hula Festival on Oahu, we train hard. It's like the Merrie Monarch for kids, you have to be invited. The first time we went, I knew the parents were saying, "When this is done, I'm taking my child out of this halau." We competed and did a clean sweep of all the categories we entered. Then the parents asked when practice was going to start up again! Now the parents say, "Lei, thank you so much because my daughter is so responsible, she's so respectful in all areas of life." Hula teaches them about commitment, about working hard and not giving up.

My mom has missed out on a lot of what I have accomplished, because she passed away right after I started my halau and before my children were born. But I truly believe that she is my angel in Heaven. I think there's a line up there where you ask for special favors and I think my mom keeps on cutting in line, because I've received so many blessings over the past few years. And the blessings just keep on coming.

Salt of the Earth

Kuulei Santos

Hawaiian families have been making salt by hand at the salt pans near Salt Pond Beach in Hanapepe for generations in a labor-intensive process that is said to be the only one of its type in the world, dating back to when the island was first inhabited.

The Santos ohana (family) works the salt flats every year along with 17 other families. Everyone participates regardless of their age; it's not uncommon to see relatives in their 70s, 80s and 90s happily doing the most grueling parts of the labor, as they have done since they were children.

Kuulei Santos, 37, reflects on the joy of keeping a cultural tradition alive, why, after months of toil, her family gives away the salt they have made, and about protecting the fragile Salt Pond area for future generations.

We Make Salt Out of Love

My grandmother, Sarah Loa, spoke Hawaiian, played ukulele and sang hundreds of Hawaiian songs by memory. She made Hawaiian quilts, feather hat bands and shell leis. She passed on before I was able to learn any of those talents. But the one skill that she taught my father, that he taught me, and that I have now passed onto my children is making salt at the Hanapepe salt flats.

Every summer I get to stand in the same spot my grandmother stood, the same spot my father stood when he was a child, and I create paakai *(salt)*. It is hard work, but we make salt out of love: love for our culture, love for our history and for our family members who are working alongside us. Out of that love comes a gift that our family has always given away or traded for other things. Why not keep that part of the tradition alive?

Salt is very old world. It balances our modern lives of cars, TV, working to support a family. When we're making salt, we get to slow down. There are no cell phones, no radios, just working side by side with each other. There is lots of laughter, lots of stories and lots of affection.

Making salt the old way is backbreaking labor. You're on your hands and knees in the hot sun. The next day you're in so much pain, your body is so sore. You have to scrub your body for two days to get the black clay out of your pores. Normally I don't like mud, I don't like to get dirty. I like to get my fingernails and toenails painted. But when I'm at the salt patch, I'm a totally different person. I get dirty, my nails get ruined. But I don't care. I just love it, where it came from, who taught it to me and why I teach it to my children. I enjoy every moment of it.

Growing up I couldn't see the importance of going to the salt patch every summer. I rebelled when I was in high school. I always came up with an excuse why I didn't want to go. When I had my first daughter, I realized the importance of connecting her with our culture.

Ever since both my girls learned to walk, I made sure they experienced salt-making every summer, no excuses. They both love paakai season and they understand that teaching what they know is how we are going to keep our culture alive. They have been assigned tasks. The older one is the photographer and she does a great job documenting the process to share online. The smaller one likes to get really dirty, then she has a reason to run to the ocean to clean off.

Salt-Making

The salt-making season usually starts in June. The first step each year is that the men jump into the seven to eight-feet deep earthen wells that were covered by the ocean all winter, and bail out all the water. Then they scrub the sides to open the pores so the ocean that seeps underground can flow into the wells.

At the same time, we begin preparing the shallow punee (*beds*) by scraping out mud that built up during the winter, and start lining the pans with thick, gooey black clay. We get down on our hands and knees to shape the clay by hand, smoothing it first with rough rocks, then progressively smoother rocks. Getting the consistency of the clay just right is important because if the clay doesn't bind together, the pan walls will crack and we have to start over.

Once the clay dries, we fill the punee with ocean water from the wells. The water crystallizes into salt flakes and forms layers. My father adds water every two or three days until the salt layers are thick. Then we harvest, wash the salt, and bring it home to dry on tables. We harvest every three or four weeks all summer until the rains come. Each harvest fills 15 to 20 small metal buckets. In a good summer, we have about six harvests.

Some people say the secret to Hanapepe salt's sweet taste is in the brine shrimp that live in the wells. When you have brine shrimp in the wells, that's when you know you're going to have a good season.

Frank Santos, Kuulei's father, applying the clay to make a punee (bed)
where the salt from ocean water will crystallize.
(Photo courtesy Kuulei Santos)

Help us Protect this Little Area

Traditionally, the families who are salt-makers have been humble. They don't talk about what they do inside the salt patch. But I started realizing that we've got to say something to protect what we have.

If you look at Hanapepe from above, the salt patch is in the middle. We're surrounded by a county park, the airport and former sugar plantation land. People drive on the sand and drive through our parking lot, spraying sand and asphalt into our clay, making it hard to bind properly. People will sometimes throw their bottles into the parking lot and break glass that ends up in the salt patch.

It is important to teach everyone that their actions affect the salt. The more people understand, the more people will respect what we have here and will help us protect this little area so we can save this tradition.

That's why I began giving tours of the salt patch to schoolchildren and visitors. When people see for themselves the full extent of what goes into making salt and the love we have for this process, they are amazed.

There's a fine line between old Hawaii and new Hawaii. As long as Hawaiian people keep some traditions alive and pass down some part of our culture to our children, the Hawaiian culture will always be a part of them. It will stay alive.

Quilting Hawaiian-Style

Jane Vegas

Jane Vegas was born and raised on Kauai, and still lives in the house her husband built for their family in 1942. She learned to find respite from a horrible childhood in her love for sewing, eventually becoming a respected and sought-after Hawaiian quilt-maker and instructor who is now celebrated at quilting shows and workshops.

Hawaiian quilting is an art form that has evolved over 200 years, characterized by a graceful geometric appliqué pattern of leaves, flowers or fruit surrounded by quilting stitched "echo-style," rippling out from the design. The appliqué is cut from a single piece of folded fabric like the snowflakes children make from paper in school. Prized for their beauty and history, many Hawaiian quilts are held in private collections and museums. The patience and skills required to sew a Hawaiian quilt are possessed by very few: a full-size quilt can take more than 1,000 hours to complete.

Jane, 88, speaks softly in a blend of standard English and Pidgin English, switching back and forth between past and present tense while recalling past events. She looks back on her life and the joy that making Hawaiian quilts has always given her

I lived on Kauai all my life. My grandparents came from Puerto Rico. My mother was born on Kauai. I had two brothers. The other siblings all died when they were babies. My oldest sister was one year old when she died. The other two, I don't know how old they were when they died. I don't know what they died from. Must be pneumonia or something.

I lived in Kukuiula Camp from when I was nine to 19 years old among Portuguese, Japanese and Filipinos. Most parents worked for McBryde Sugar Company. I used to mix more with the Japanese girls. They were very nice and they wanted to learn things so I used to help them and they used to help me. We used to play with mud, make all kinds of pretend food. There were a lot of girls in the camp. We didn't have to mingle with the boys.

My childhood was bad. My father was always fighting with my mother. That's all I can remember. My father was a romantic guy. He liked to fool around, and he didn't want her to go and do the same thing that he was doing so they used to fight, always.

After her mother was murdered by her father, Jane lived with her maternal grandparents who were lost in bitterness over their daughter's death, taking it out unpleasantly on their grandchildren.

My grandparents, they were sometimes good with me and sometimes they used to call me names. I had fun only on Sundays. We used to run away with the girls and we used to go to Lawai Beach. I couldn't swim because I was afraid of my grandfather. He used to tell me, "If I catch you in the water, I'm going to spank you." So I never did learn to swim. We'd just put our feet in the water, that's all.

I started working in the sugar fields when I was 11 years old during the summer, kalai (*hoeing*), weeding the sugar cane, for 10 cents an hour, eight hours a day. We wore regular pants and long-sleeved shirts with a hat fo' shade from sun, and a cloth alongside our face and under our chins. We worked all Kukuiula, the hills and everything for McBryde.

We didn't know how to work, we wanted to make fast (*be done quickly*). Since we leave some of the grass back, they call us back and tell us, "You gotta pull more weeds out from the cane, gotta pull out more of the grass."

When we used to work in the sugar cane fields we used to exchange food. They used to like my Puerto Rican food and I used to exchange for their Japanese food. My grandmother used to make beef stew and sometimes Vienna sausage with fried egg. The Japanese food was good. They tell me, "Try put water in your rice and make like a soup." I made it. Oh, I can't eat this! I had to throw my rice away.

Jane was required to give her entire paycheck to her grandmother, who would return $5 to her. In 1938, after she graduated from 8th grade, Jane put a $5 down payment on a Singer treadle sewing machine at Kukuiula Store, a nearby general store, and took it home. Every month she paid $5 more toward the sewing machine's purchase price of more than $200. When she married at 19 years old, her husband paid off the balance.

I worked for the sugar plantation until I was 12 and I didn't want to work in the fields any more. Then I went to look for maid job. The ladies were sometimes mean. We want to do work so we had to take it what they tell us to do. I just do my job and forget, let them talk. I worked as maid around four years, then I didn't want to work anymore.

I stayed home and tried to do some sewing. I knew how to crochet so I wanted to know how to sew dresses. Me and this girlfriend who lived across the street, we said, "Let's go try." Oh, it came out good. Sometimes dresses come out little bit crooked but then we take it off and fix it up again. We used to cut on newspaper the patterns that we liked. We looked at books and made our own, mostly dresses for us. We tried to make kimonos but didn't come out good.

I used to see my friend Elizabeth do Hawaiian quilting. I tell her, "I wonder if I can learn how to do this?" She tell me, "Oh, yeah, you can learn but nobody fo' teach you, because that's our tradition to learn and we don't want to teach anybody." I told my husband, "Oh, I wish I could know how to make quilt."

In 1960, Jane phoned Hannah Baker, a revered Hawaiian quilt-maker and instructor at the University of Hawaii on Oahu, who agreed to come to Kauai and teach if Jane assembled a group of 15 ladies. Jane assembled 16 women plus herself for the classes.

Hannah Baker came and she taught us four times. Only learned how to cut the pattern and lay out and how to place it, that's all. Never learned how to quilt. I looked at the books and I used to go to the stores and I used to see ready-made quilts and I tell, "I wonder how they make this?" I used to come home and my stitches were half an inch big. Supposed to be tiny but I didn't know that yet. I used to fill up every corner of the quilt.

Over time, Jane taught herself the finer points of Hawaiian quilt-making from books and keenly observing others, finally mastering the art when she was 42 years old. She knew she had found her calling.

Jane became engrossed in quilting, often sewing for eight hours each day — a king-size Hawaiian quilt can take about six months to complete. In short order, her quilts were sought after and she became in demand as a quilting instructor. Other quilters, finding the craft took too long, asked her to complete quilts they had started. She continued

*Jane Vegas with her original sewing machine that she
bought in 1938 after she graduated from 8th grade.
(Photo by Pamela Varma Brown)*

*using her original sewing machine that she had purchased in 1938 —
converted to electric along the way — until 2009, making clothes for
her children and more than 1,000 quilts of all sizes.*

*Today, Jane sews by hand, her daughter, Cathy Counts, completing
her work on a newer electric machine. In 2005, Jane was featured in
a Japanese quilting magazine. In 2010 and 2012 she was an honored
guest at quilting shows on Kauai's North Shore.*

I used to quilt every day. Sometimes I used to go to sleep at 3
o'clock in the morning because I was quilting. If I had my allergy
in the night I'd come out to the living room and quilt. Sometimes I
forget to cook and my kids tell me, "We're not going to eat tonight?"
and I had to stop and go and cook. I wanted to see how it feels when

I get finished with the quilt.

I used to do it as a business, so I had to go take license. I didn't want to work but the ladies wanted to learn how to quilt and they knew I knew how. They pay me $8 an hour to learn and it was two-hour classes. I started working with the seniors first at the neighborhood centers. So I used to be in Koloa Mondays, Tuesday Waimea, Wednesday Kapaa, Thursday Hanapepe and Friday Lihue. I even teach my eighth grade teacher. I was nervous to teach her because she was my teacher when I was young. She was a good student.

I never learn to drive until I was 65. My husband passed away and I get no way for go out or grocery store or teach my classes, so I had to learn. I started on a Datsun, a small little station wagon. My son tell me, "You can learn with this one. It's an old car so if you smash 'em, it's OK."

One day I went with my lady friend, before I take my license. I had permit only. She took me to Salt Pond and she made me drive all through the steep hills coming down, back of Kalaheo. I tell her, "I don't have brakes." I tell her but she never hear me or something. We went to the post office and came back and she tell me, "You don't have brakes." I said, "I've been telling you from Kalaheo we don't have brakes on the car!" God was with us because I didn't get anything happen to us coming down that steep hill.

When I first drive by myself, I was nervous. When I used to drive to Kapaa and come back, my nerves was all jumping. I have to lie down and relax after I come home.

Jane expanded her talents to using Hawaiian quilt-making techniques on more modern thematic designs for family members, including outlining printed elements from colorful sarongs and using them as the appliqué, and embellishing dolphin-shaped appliqués with French knots for eyes. Recently she spotted a photo of a crocheted tablecloth with a butterfly and heart motif in a Japanese book and copied it, creating a beautiful, lace-like gift for a friend in Puerto Rico. "I no can read Japanese but I look at the pictures," she says. Over the years, Jane taught hundreds of students the art of sewing Hawaiian quilts, many of whom are Hawaii residents and some who were vacationing on Kauai.

Jane Vegas with her husband of 47 years, Solomon.
(Photo courtesy of Jane Vegas)

Sometimes I see my students. They say, "I remember you." When they say they know me, I feel happy inside.

I have seven children, 18 grandchildren, 28 great-grandchildren and two great-great grandchildren. I don't remember all their names. I mix them all up. I'm calling one, I'm calling everyone. They all look at me, "Who you like talk to?"

Now I work on my sewing and on my crocheting.

I just want to quilt, that's all. Just to see it finished. I feel happy when I make a Hawaiian quilt.

*Jane Vegas sits in front of the quilt she made for her daughter,
Cathy Counts, when Cathy was married in 1968. The quilt is named
"Haleakala Highway" because it depicts the Silver Sword and other
flowers one might see while driving up to Maui's Haleakala volcano.
(Photo by Pamela Varma Brown)*

Toro Nagashi
By Jean Rhude

One of the many pleasures of living on Kauai is being welcomed to experience traditions of many cultures. In Japanese tradition, the Bon or Obon Festival is a time when spirits of the departed come to visit loved ones. On the last day of the festival, paper lanterns containing small lighted candles are set adrift upon the ocean or rivers, to help guide the spirits back home. This ceremony, named toro nagashi, is a beautiful and touching sight to behold as dozens or more lanterns and their soft golden glow float gently away.

Jean Rhude, a writer and grandmother on Kauai, shares the reverence and beauty of toro nagashi through the wonderment of both her own and a child's eyes.

The young boy's blue eyes sparkle as he watches from atop his father's shoulders. At about five years of age he is aware of the solemnity of the event. This is a different feeling than when the boy and his father launch their kayak or picnic on the riverbank. Even the lights strung through the park alongside Wailua River seem to know better than to appear festive on this night. The ringing bells and clanging cymbals carry a resonance of seriousness. There is no formal program, just a quiet surrender to the unfolding of the event. The coconut wireless has sent her silent message and I am both a participant and observer in this ancient Japanese tradition.

This ceremony, called toro nagashi, takes place at the end of Bon or Obon season, a time in the Japanese culture when the living are reunited with the spirits of their ancestors and other loved ones. Toro nagashi helps the spirits of loved ones return to their own world.

The mostly Japanese participants at this ceremony at Wailua River welcome everyone of other cultures, including Hawaiians, Caucasians, Portuguese and other Asians, who make up the crowd of about 150 people. A portable altar is faced so the priest can look out to the river as he chants and lights a candle. A line forms and members of the Jodo Buddhist Temple bow before the altar as they pass in single file, dipping their fingers into a bowl of water. It reminds me of taking communion.

Several participants walk to the hundred or so lanterns that are attached with a decorative lotus blossom to a series of five barges, and begin to light each one individually. Each lantern is inscribed with the name of someone who has died, for whom it honors. About 20 more lanterns are placed in each barge and each barge slipped into the water, where they are pulled so as not to pollute the river with fuel. The illumination of the lanterns is immediately intensified by their reflection in the water. The full moon shines through the swaying palm trees.

Slowly the barges move up the river and then are brought back down where they pass the crowd of people on the shore. We are mostly holding hands or hugging. Young children perch on the sea wall holding small paper lanterns attached to sticks with candles inside that their tutus (*grandmothers*) have brought them. They sit and watch in silence, dangling their feet just above the water. The fragrance of incense fills the air.

I stand holding the hand of my sister and we silently contemplate the lanterns we have purchased for our mother and for my son.

We do not know which of the lanterns in the water floats their names but this is not important in the glow of their collective light. I consider the healing represented by grieving in this way, with strangers, whose shared experience is stronger than our separateness. We share in the glow of that mingled light in a celebration of our collective love of our ancestors. It feels good to create ceremony here on this island of Kauai that has become my home.

The sweet boy with blond curls and blue eyes listens closely as his father explains to him, "The candles are for peoples' family members who have died. The candles light their way." "Their way to where daddy?" His father gently replies, "On their way to eternity."

Aloha is Love
Kelvin Ho

Kelvin Ho performs blessings, weddings and ceremonies of passage. Though people refer to him as a kahu (minister), he eschews formal labels, guided instead by opportunities to be of service. A resident of Kauai for more than 30 years, moving from Oahu when he was in his early 20s, Kelvin speaks thoughtfully about aloha, the specialness of Kauai and understanding the island's host culture.

Aloha is what your heart feels like when you share. Aloha is love. It's the absence of fear. It's a lifestyle, a way to live.

One of my teachers taught me, "When the Divine first tasted the lips of what it was like to be Hawaiian, it expressed and sang forth as aloha."

One thing that people feel deeply on Kauai is our practice of aloha aina *(taking care of the land)*. In the Hawaiian spiritual path, nature isn't seen as the creation of the Divine but literally the body form of the Divine, and mountainous regions and upland forests are wao akua *(realm of the gods)*. It is said the Divine flows through water that comes down from the highest. When we malama the aina *(take care of the land)*, we are one with the Divine. In this belief, you are in a moment-to-moment dance with the Divine through nature. There is a great wisdom in harmonizing with nature because it's not something separate from you. It's who you are.

When you love a place, it's natural you want to care for it. That's what Hawaiians have always done. It's important to honor and learn as much as possible from our host culture, one that lived in a fully sustainable way for so many generations. Anytime that we're guests anywhere, that's always the respectful way.

I grew up all my life in Hawaii, in the city on Oahu, but I never felt like I experienced the depth of the spirit of any of the islands until I came to Kauai. Arriving here was a real awakening for me because of what's here, but also what's not here. Living on Kauai was my first step into a rural lifestyle, an abundance of resources, to be in uncrowded surf, to see fish and wildlife all around.

Kauai has always been different from the other Hawaiian islands. There's something here that touches people's spirits, a healing. It's always mind-boggling what similar experiences that people of all different ages, cultures and backgrounds speak of when talking about their time on Kauai.

When you stay here for a time, you become part of the community and it becomes very natural to want to serve and to connect and to give. That's so much more fulfilling for everybody, because that's part of aloha. That's who we are.

Sharing is Aloha
Phil Villatora

Phil Villatora was born and raised on Kauai, the eighth of 13 children. His parents taught by example about aloha, respect, sustainability and harmony. He shares these values with his 70 nieces and nephews, 24 grandnieces and grandnephews, and visitors on Kauai.

As founder of Na Keiki o Ka Aina (Children of the Land) Polynesian Cultural Center on Kauai, Phil helps keep Polynesian culture alive through classes, arts, performances and the sharing of aloha with people of all ages.

The concept of aloha is appreciation. For example, from the minute you give someone a lei, whether that lei is made from flowers or seashells, you set the intention of aloha.

Aloha is also the understanding that you'll get more respect when you give respect.

Aloha is really two words: alo means to be in the presence of; ha is your breath. So aloha means taking the time to be present with someone, to take a deep breath, to play some music, to enjoy your life.

In my family, we show aloha to my mother. We don't celebrate our birthdays. Instead we celebrate Labor Day. It's her day and we bring her gifts.

I grew up in a place called Puhi Camp in one of the houses provided by Grove Farm Company for employees of their sugar plantation, where my father worked for 43 years as a crane operator. Grove Farm gave our family extra land to grow pigs, goats, cows, chickens, ducks, bananas and a garden that we shared with other families. They knew my dad needed land to feed his kids and to help others. That showed aloha.

Our family has always known that more than words, sharing is aloha.

Aloha with Your Newspaper
By Lincoln Henry Gill

Lincoln Gill is a real estate broker who moved to Kauai from Colorado in 2010, yearning for the feel of a small community that he experienced growing up in Rochester, Minnesota. He found it on the Garden Island.

One Sunday morning I cut down a large bunch of bananas from one of our trees. It was huge, about 120 bananas, far more than we could eat ourselves or freeze to use later. I split the bananas into smaller bunches and placed them in a box where our driveway meets the street. I attached a sign to the box announcing they were "FREE!"

Throughout that day, I looked out my window and smiled as people drove by, helping themselves to bananas. I just love how people on Kauai share their extra fruit. We are fortunate that our trees produce more than enough to give away.

By the end of the day there were still a couple of bunches remaining. I left the box on the side of the road in case anyone coming home from working the night shift wanted some.

Two mornings later, when I put my hand into our narrow daily newspaper receptacle, I got a surprise. There was a package with a note. Inside the package I found six small loaves of freshly-baked banana bread. They were still warm! The note read:

*This is in appreciation for the bananas which
you shared last night. Enjoy!
Your Garden Island newspaper carriers,
Robert and Winona Romero*

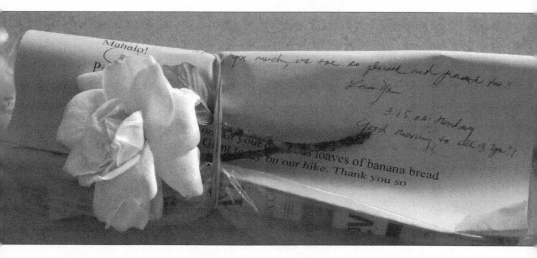

That was out of left field! When you leave fruit out for people to take, as people do on Kauai all the time, you don't expect to hear from anyone. You just know they are enjoying it. The scenario was even more amazing because we had not known who our newspaper carriers were. They used to deliver the paper around 4 or 5 in the morning while we were still sleeping.

The banana bread was absolutely delicious, with walnuts and small bits of fresh coconut. Every few bites I kept thinking, "Wow, that's amazing! I never expected to get banana bread. How thoughtful of them."

The next time I cut down a bunch of bananas, I set aside a dozen for the Romeros and put them in a plastic bag near our newspaper receptacle. Sure enough, a few days later, they delivered another batch of freshly-baked mini loaves of banana bread with our newspaper. This batch had tiny chocolate bits inside — delicious again!

We continued to leave bananas for them periodically as our trees produced. One time they even left a gardenia blossom with our newspaper and banana bread. The aloha spirit makes you want to pass it on.

Eventually we met Robert and Winona face-to-face and found out they are even sweeter in person. And we still exchange bananas for banana bread. Now that we know them, we wave or stop and say "Hi" when we see them delivering papers.

It's because of people like Robert and Winona Romero that I like life in a small town. On Kauai we get it with fresh bananas and aloha.

Winona and Robert Romero, ages 79 and 74, respectively.
(Photo by Pamela Varma Brown)

Aloha at the Grocery Store
By Elizabeth Suenaga

Liz Suenaga grew up on Oahu, was a teacher in public schools for 30 years in California, and is now happily enjoying retirement on Kauai.

I see bumper stickers that read, "Live Aloha" or "Got Aloha?" What does this truly mean? I watched it one day at the grocery store.

The check-out line that day was surprisingly long, but I thought, "What the heck. Relax. Lucky you live Kauai."

At that moment, a teenager at the front of the line turned around and waved his arms to an elderly Japanese woman standing in front of me. "Auntie-san, come. Bring your stuff." (*"San" is a Japanese title of respect.*)

The young man got out of line, helped take the woman's items out of her shopping basket and placed them on the conveyor belt.

This simple gesture is what it's like to "Live Aloha." People on Kauai do this every day.

Everything Makes a Beautiful Memory

Fanny Bilodeau

Artist Fanny Bilodeau captures the warmth and beauty of Kauai with her colorful paintings of tropical fruit and flowers that are luscious enough to pluck from the canvas, beach scenes that invite you to jump into turquoise ocean water and rustic sugar plantation camp houses from a bygone era. Bringing her whimsical side out to play, Fanny also depicts Kauai's many wild chickens with their lovely plumage as they play stringed instruments, surf, barbecue corn and other human-like activities.

Born in Zaire, Fanny attended school in Belgium, lived in the southern United States and also the state of Washington before moving to the Garden Island in the 1990s. Bubbly, laughing easily and often, Fanny talks about the joy of painting on Kauai and her journey to becoming a full-time artist.

The lifestyle on Kauai is a wonderful, slow pace. You can stop and examine the petals on a flower and enjoy yourself for awhile. In other places it's "hurry, hurry, hurry," and you miss out on life. When you're an old person lying in your bed and you know you're going to die, you will think, "Why didn't I stop and look and breathe things in and enjoy my life? Why did I hurry so hard?" We've got to slow down to really enjoy life.

On Kauai I am inspired by everything: the air, the sounds, the warmth, the people. Sometimes I turn a corner while driving and bam, there it is! Other times it's a color or the texture that I want to see if I can make happen on canvas. There's life everywhere you look. Just stop and look at the color of the mangoes or a plumeria blossom. What you feel is what you paint. Even smells can get put on canvas. Everything makes a beautiful memory.

One of my favorite places to paint on Kauai is the Waimea Plantation Cottages (*57 authentic sugar plantation camp houses that have been renovated and are now vacation rentals*). They have so much character, each one is different. The stories those cottages could tell you are inspiring. I first went to paint a couple, and then a couple more, then they wanted to carry my paintings on the property. So I just went crazy for awhile and painted the cottages. While I was painting them, I'd meet people who would tell me, "Oh, that was my house," and they would share their stories about living there.

My paintings of the cottages sold great. I thought I would do more of them, but then the chickens happened.

I'll Never Stop Painting Chickens

When I first started painting chickens, I didn't know if the paintings were going to sell well or not. It turns out, people just connect with them. I'm so happy because I would do them just for me for fun. Some of the gallery owners say they can hear people walking through their galleries, then start laughing, and they know their customers have come to my chicken paintings. We all need that laughter.

People always ask where all the chickens on Kauai came from.

You've got to come up with an answer, so I thought, "Well, they all came on the 'Chicken Express,'" so I painted "Chicken Express" that shows a flock of chickens sailing themselves ashore on a beach on Kauai.

In my painting "Hens Misbehaving," a wiener dog is driving a minibus full of hens that are all misbehaving at Hanalei Bay. One of them is plopping an egg out the window, another one is watching to see if it's going to crack and roll. Two of them are hooting at a rooster who is highly annoyed. A chicken on the roof of the bus is already wearing his snorkel, and there's a little wagon full of chicks in the back.

When I have a good thought about a chicken painting, I can't wait to get onto that. The thing is, they don't pose for you. They've got all these goofy moves so you have to think about how do their legs work? How am I going to make this realistic? In "Spring Chickens," that shows six roosters and two hens flying up in the sky with springs under their feet, one is doing a big ballet move, almost like the splits. Chickens don't really do that. I get to use my imagination to make my paintings fun.

I also like painting mynah birds. They are such little hoodlums; they're so naughty. You always see them scrapping on the side of the road and making trouble. "The Imposter" is a painting of a mynah bird wearing a bright red rooster comb on his head, trying to fake like he's a rooster. The funny thing is, some of the people who have bought that art have not understood that he's not a chicken, he's a mynah bird, even though you can see his rooster comb is held on by a chin strap. It makes me laugh.

While I'm painting the chickens and mynah birds, the real part of me gets to come out, not just the serious artist. There's this little stinker side of me. I just think of these things all the time. I'll never stop painting chickens.

Your Dreams Can Come True

Ever since I was a young child, I have been fascinated with detail: the texture of a petal or leaf between my fingers, how a plant moves in the breeze, what things look like in different types of light. I look at everything until I have memories that are beyond sight; they become experiences that have emotional depth.

My grandfather and my great grandfather were both artists and we always had art around us growing up. My father was always very supportive of my art talents. When I was seven, we moved to America and I began doodling all the time, like even when our family played games like Monopoly while I was waiting for my turn. I did artwork all the way through high school.

My husband, Ron, and I got married out of high school and we had four kids. From then it was all about taking care of the children. As our kids got a little bit older and I had a bit more time, I created a little line of cards in black and white, in pen and ink and pencil. People were actually buying them.

Then a card company from California saw my line and they wanted it! They flew me from Washington, where we lived, to California and gave me a color-rendering class which was a whole semester smashed into two hours. It just about blew my mind. I learned so much about how to render in color. My whole art changed at that point. There were so many things I would never have thought of, like how you shade colors. For example, what would you shade yellow with? It's whatever's opposite on the color wheel. If I want to shade a lemon yellow, I might add a little white for highlights, but underneath, I'll want to put a little purple. It's opposite on the color wheel to the yellow and it will be the perfect color. On the orange you'd want to put a little bit of blue; on the red there would be a little bit of green. It's just amazing how that works so well. If every artist knew that, all their art would pop.

When we came to Kauai, the kids were in their teenage years and taking care of themselves a little bit more. One day Ron and I saw some of artist James Coleman's pieces in a gallery, little bougainvillea-covered cottages. I remember we wanted one so badly, but it cost around $4,500. They said you could pay $100 bucks a month until you pay it off. I had some old paints and I thought, "I'm just going to try and do one the best I can," and it came out good! And somebody bought it for $50. I did another one and somebody bought it for $75. I couldn't believe it! It just kind of got me started because I was loving doing it anyway. It was like playing and getting paid for it.

At one point, when I was working at a Wyland art gallery, I met James Coleman. I asked him, "How do we get really good at painting? How do we get to the next level?" He said, "Fanny, you're never going to get good sitting here selling my art. You need to quit your job, go home and paint." I asked Ron, "Is that do-able?" He said, "Sure, come on home and paint." So I did, and I really got good faster.

It was a little bit scary. I thought, "What about if I can't? What if this doesn't work out? What if people hate my art?" But I was going to give it a good try. Almost right away we made a few prints, 12 at first. When those 12 sold, I took the money and made 24. When those 24 sold, I did 48. And I just kept going.

All of a sudden you start hitting all these plateaus and it starts coming easier and faster and better. You just surprise yourself. It's amazing how we're hard-wired to do that.

*Fanny Bilodeau (with friend) captures the warmth
and whimsy of Kauai in her paintings.
(Photo courtesy Ron Bilodeau)*

After awhile, I realized, "Wow, I'm making this much. Maybe we can just simplify and Ron could work with me and help me put the art out to stores and galleries." That took it to another level. I couldn't do it myself. Ron, who had been such a hard-working man, who allowed me to stay at home most of the time, raise those four kids and paint, now we get to work together. He's such a nice man; we always get along.

Now every day is filled with what I love. I just get so excited that I can't wait to paint the next picture.

The main thing for people who want to make a go of what they love is just getting past the not knowing what to do. Just feel it, do it. That's all getting good is. You *will* be good. It will take X amount of time. And if it's hard, just get past that. Just look at where you want to be and start walking to that place, that's all you do. One thing I've learned: You'll get there.

When you learn that you can be whatever you want to be, all of a sudden you realize there are no stoppers. It will come, if you can just have fun doing it. If you just realize that, your dreams can come true, be it painting or whatever you want to do.

Tasting Kauai
By Marta Lane

Marta Lane moved to Kauai in 2010 to launch her new career as a food writer, after 25 years working as a video editor in Colorado. An energetic, bubbly woman with a passion for all kinds of food, beer and wine, she was welcomed into the island's culinary and farming communities with open arms.

Marta writes about restaurants, breweries and all things food, with an emphasis on farms and farmers. She also shares recipes, arranges food tours and has an insider's scoop on Kauai's food scene.

The first time I vacationed on Kauai, I was shy about trying the exotic produce that filled the stalls at the farmers market. Eating a papaya was the most adventurous I got. We didn't have those in Colorado. Today, papaya, with its juicy flesh, delicate flavor and floral scent is one of my favorite Kauai fruits.

Living on Kauai and writing about the island's farmers has introduced me to a wide variety of tantalizing fruits and vegetables. More importantly, it has opened my eyes to an artful way of living. Before I moved here, I knew that produce grown on small, family farms was labor-intensive because these farmers work with nature, rather than against it. But until I tried it myself, I had no idea how much work farming actually is.

Two months after I moved to Kauai, I took a 12-week organic farming class in Kilauea taught by veteran farmer Jillian Seals, a young dynamo, who also cares for four children and her husband. We students were obliged to work on the farm for 10 hours every week and attend lessons for five hours each week.

I was the new kid in town and Jillian was a buoy that kept me from floating away on an ocean of self-doubt. It was at her farm, among friendship, laughter and music that I learned about aloha, planted the seeds for a new career and got a peek into the art of farming.

Jillian grows food in three 5,000 square-foot gardens, each a square patch filled with rows of progressively smaller concentric circles. A path bisects the length and width of each garden, dividing it into four quarters.

Jillian uses one garden to teach children how to grow and cook food. The keiki *(children)* sharpen their math skills by weighing harvests and measuring decomposing compost piles. The other two are production gardens whose yields fill restaurant and grocery store coolers, along with weekly Community Supported Agriculture (CSA) boxes for consumers who want to eat freshly-picked produce from local farms.

Our class started in a big, red barn where Jillian would ask how the gardens looked. In the beginning, we didn't take notice. Later, armed with clipboards and pencils, we followed her into the gardens where we examined the plants that didn't look healthy, noting which section they were in, what types of bugs were on or near the plants, and if the plants were weepy, full of holes or brown in color. Today, my eyes automatically scan a farmer's garden, noting its health with a quick glance.

The romance of working in a garden filled with birdsong, balmy weather, rustling coconut palms and the sound of waves crashing into the nearby cliffs quickly faded. My legs were achy and restless as

I spent hours squatting over rows of hand-tilled dirt, pulling weeds or planting hundreds of seedlings. The heat radiating off the red soil that stained my hands caused sweat to trickle into my eyes.

I later learned that Kauai's North Shore has the heaviest concentration of the island's organic farmers. They don't grow organically because the label brings them higher prices; small farms barely cover their operating costs. They do it because they believe that protecting delicate ecosystems, the land, sea and people from chemical pesticides and fertilizers is the right thing to do.

One cold and rainy morning, we were harvesting for the farm's CSA and wholesale accounts, and for produce to bring to the first anniversary party of the Mayor's Aloha Garden in Lihue. The mayor's garden promotes agriculture on Kauai, and is maintained by volunteers who plant and harvest the produce that is donated to local charities.

If we were on our game, it would take us five hours to do the job. We'd start at 7 a.m., and by noon we'd be finished harvesting, washing, sorting and packing produce, cleaning the wash station, feeding the plants and cultivating the beds.

On this particular day, the rain was non-stop. The steady stream of water made the paths muddy, our shoes sucking with every step. Our clothes were wetter than just-washed and our hair stuck to our heads. But we finished, changed into clean clothes and arrived in time to hear the mayor sing an emotional rendition of "Beautiful Kauai" at the anniversary celebration. Everything on Kauai is intertwined in such a beautiful way.

One hot summer day, we were sweltering in the barn listening to the post-lunch lecture. We were learning about sustainable irrigation methods (catching rainwater in 50-gallon barrels and using ponds as a resource for seasons of drought), and the hard, plastic chairs did little to keep us awake. We were doing our best to answer a question

Jillian had asked, when a man named Huy came with a delivery of bulky green coconuts.

Half of the class, including me, had never tasted the refreshing nectar of a fresh coconut, so Jillian decided to treat us. Shuffling from the dim barn into the bright midday sun, we clustered under the canopy of a large, wide tree where Huy opened the young coconuts with a machete and handed one to each of us.

I held the coconut with both hands and tipped the small opening to my lips. A sweet, cool liquid filled my mouth. I was surprised that it didn't contain the creamy, milky stuff in cans that I had been sure filled their shells. I have since learned that coconut water is loaded with electrolytes, making it an all-natural Gatorade.

Branching Out

Since attending that farming class, I have tried many exotic Kauai fruits. Winter brings rambutan, a round fruit with hairy red skin that protects its grape-like flesh. Springtime is longan season. You can easily crack their hard, brown shells and quench your thirst with the luscious, almost nutty-flavored fruit. Lychee, a round succulent fruit, is like the offspring of a rambutan and longan: smaller than the former, and bigger than the latter, the skin is red like a rambutan, and smooth like a longan. The delicate flesh is the perfume of tropical summer and one I look forward to every year.

Perhaps the most alien-looking thing I have tried is the mildly sweet dragon fruit. It's about the size of a man's fist, with neon pink skin, and pointy green leaves. These cactus fruit bloom under moonlight and fruit from late July to October. At $6 to $8 each, they are pricy but worth it. Their fragile white flesh, almost like a watermelon, and crisp kiwi-like seeds, are exquisite. I like to chill them in the

Rambutan have sweet grape-like flesh inside.

refrigerator, cut them in half and eat them with a spoon.

Kauai's year-round growing season means farmers markets are always bursting with a colorful selection of sweet and juicy fruit. I buy mangos, pineapple and mountain apples in the summer; apple bananas and papayas in the fall; a rainbow of citrus in the winter; chocolate sapote in the spring; and star fruit and avocado from fall through winter. If you're at the market and you see a strange looking fruit, be brave and try a sample. Farmers are happy to share.

My husband and I have been to more than 80 farms on Kauai, and I am grateful to those who have shown me the dedication farmers have in bringing food to our collective table.

I've interviewed farmers while they have looked at acres of watermelon, devastated by wild pigs. I've talked with farmers who have figured out how to grow big, fat tomatoes, which are very difficult to cultivate on Kauai. I've learned the painstaking steps a tea farmer

Alien-looking dragon fruit is mildly sweet.
(Photo courtesy Daniel Lane/Pono Photo)

takes when harvesting and processing her specialty tea by hand.

Once, I even got to "sort" cows, sitting on a platform 10 feet in the air, my legs straddling a chute between two pens, directing immature cows to a pen on my left and mature thousand-pound cows to the pen on my right.

Kauai's farmers are strong-willed, generous and kind and they meet challenges head-on in order to feed people. Kauai's chefs adore cooking with locally-grown fruits, vegetables, beef, island-grown shrimp and locally-caught fish, and they love preparing unique dishes that delight our palates.

I've eaten a lot of great food on this island. I feel deep gratitude for the people who grow it and cook it. I am blessed to be able to share their challenges and their victories with people who enjoy good food.

Angels on Kauai
By Sue Kanoho

Sue Kanoho has been the executive director of the Kauai Visitors Bureau since 1997, where she embodies the aloha spirit of Kauai for the island's many tourists. She shares a story that illustrates how Kauai people care for visitors to the island.

In 2008, Aloha Airlines and ATA Airlines both abruptly shut down within 48 hours of each other, leaving travelers stranded in Hawaii without a ticket. Our Kauai Visitors Bureau team set up a table at Lihue Airport to help visitors find flights home and also to help our remaining airlines with their long lines.

An elderly man was flustered and was having a hard time remembering things. He had flown into Kauai on a different airline than his wife did. She had already flown home to return to her job.

I helped the gentleman get a flight from Kauai to Oahu, where his flight home would depart from, a hotel room for his overnight stay on Oahu, and a taxi to take him to and from the airport. He was clearly worried, not knowing anyone on Oahu. He called me a few times and I reassured him he was going to be fine. All our partners looked out for him.

He got home safe and sound, and was very grateful.

A few weeks later, I received a very nice card from him, thanking his "angels" on Kauai for helping him get home.

We were happy to help. We only did what we would have wanted anyone to do, had he been our own grandpa.

Reopening Polihale
Bruce Pleas and Andy Johnston

Polihale State Park on Kauai's western shore is a seven-mile stretch of pristine white sand beach, framed on one side by world-class waves for surfing and on the other side by dramatic cliffs. The beach is an extremely popular destination for residents who enjoy the ocean or camping under a canopy of stars at night, and for visitors who appreciate its stunning beauty.

When a section of the rutted four-mile dirt access road to Polihale was completely washed out by torrential rains in 2008, the state's Department of Land and Natural Resources told the public that it would take at least two years and millions of dollars to reopen the road. Finding that unacceptable, dedicated Polihale surfers Andy Johnston and Bruce Pleas spearheaded an effort for members of the Kauai community to do the work themselves. From start to finish, an all-volunteer force of Kauai contractors and surfers, using donated machinery, completed the repairs within 10 days.

Bruce Pleas: The damage to the road to Polihale was caused by several days of rain, one day in particular in which we estimated 30 inches fell, 14 inches just in one hour. It was intense. I went out the next day to see what was going on. I got about half a mile in on the access road when I saw there was a 10-foot drop and huge hole at the end of the first bridge. The road was just gone! During the storm the bridge had clogged with debris. Water, taking its natural course, flowed around the side of the bridge, gouging the hole. There was no way to drive through.

When I first contacted our representative at the Department of Land and Natural Resources (DLNR), he told me that access to Polihale would be shut down for two years. The government made it illegal for anyone to go on the road to Polihale. What spurred us on was that they were threatening to arrest people who went out there. People were going to go to jail for going to Polihale Beach.

We attended another meeting with the DLNR when they were telling us how long it was going to take for them to fix the road. They were still talking two years. Andy got up and said, "We'll do it. We already know guys who can do the work." At first the state said, "No." But we knew we could do it.

Andy Johnston: I called KKCR, our community radio station, and said, "Here's what's going on at Polihale. The state says they can't fix the park and they're talking about keeping it closed for two years. We're talking to the state about getting a volunteer effort going to do all the work ourselves."

I hung up the phone and immediately my phone rang and it was a local guy named Myron Lindsey who had moved to Kauai from the Big Island. He said, "Hey Andy, I'm a road builder. I know how to do this stuff. I can probably free up some tractors." I took down his number. Then I called my good friend Nick Prieto, who's a surfing buddy and an excavation contractor. I was only about halfway into my explanation when he interrupted me, saying, "I'm in. When do we start?" I reminded him this was not a paid job and he said, "That's fine."

Then people started coming out of the woodwork. Contractors called other excavation contractors and we called more of our friends. From there it started mushrooming out and within a week or two we had a whole crew of guys chomping at the bit to fix the place. They had the tractors and the know-how to do it.

Polihale is a magical place to a lot of people. It's one of the most beautiful beaches on the entire planet. Everyone was willing to help.

A lot of people said, "The state is not going to let you do it." But we made personal connections at meetings with the DLNR and we came up with viable solutions so they eventually said, "Yes."

Bruce: There were about 25 companies that volunteered their time and equipment and about 40 individuals. We all worked from sunrise to sunset. About a dozen Westside eateries and individuals donated food for our volunteers.

My friend, Val Badua, graded the entire road by himself and was the main person in contact with Goodfellow Bros., the large general contractor that donated a grader and a water truck. Val has decades of experience with roads and projects such as this and made a huge difference.

We cleaned the bridge down to the concrete to inspect it for cracks and to see what kind of condition it was in. It was in great shape. The man who designed and built it in the 1950s or 1960s came out and said it was the cleanest the bridge had ever been. We even installed guardrails. Martin Steel donated prefabricated massive iron safety railings, dropped them all into place with their crane; welded them, then painted them "safety yellow."

The DLNR's engineers said the bridge had to be able to hold six tons of weight. When Martin Steel drove their 20-ton crane over it, we took a photo. I said, "Here, give this to your engineers. We already tested it." Later we had the 25-ton water truck driving on the bridge repeatedly.

From the time we started talking about doing the work ourselves until the time we were done was two months. The actual work took us only 10 days.

Andy: This became a high-profile project that got a lot of publicity. Someone put it on CNN. Rush Limbaugh even talked about it on his radio show. I didn't mind being acknowledged, but we're not heroes. There are heroes all over this island who do volunteer work every day of their lives, whether it's youth sports, or volunteering for Kauai Hospice or Kauai United Way. You'll never know their names.

There is a community spirit on Kauai that definitely comes out in times of need. It's the true meaning of the word "community." You put that many people together and things get done. It's a good feeling.

(Photo courtesy Andy Johnston)

Andy Johnston, left, and Bruce Pleas on the bridge to Polihale Beach that they were instrumental in reopening for the public.
(Photo by Pamela Varma Brown)

I Am So Blessed!

By Sadiqa Humbert

Sadiqa Humbert worked in Alaska for 20 years in the oil field construction industry, maintaining the Trans-Alaska Pipeline System for most of the year, while wintering on Kauai. Upon retirement, she moved to the island permanently where she now basks in the warmth of the sun and of Kauai's people.

The first time I walked along the shorelines of Kauai, I felt so happy I began to pray. I gave thanks for being here and I prayed for others. I felt a calm feeling and then a powerful presence with me. I wanted more.

I first visited Kauai right after Hurricane Iwa in 1982. I was amazed by the welcome I received from the most optimistic people who had just suffered devastation. I easily made friends with local people who invited me into homes and family parties, shared their local dishes, and took time to tell me about their culture. I tried and learned new things from them. I still feel the love and security of my surrogate family of Kauai residents, all a blend of different nationalities.

I was born and raised in Philadelphia, Pennsylvania. When I was 26 years old, I went to Alaska to help build and maintain the Trans-Alaska Pipeline for most of the year. The winters in Alaska were brutal. I became a "snow-bird," and came to Kauai every winter.

While here, I learned much about Hawaiian monk seals; how to pick edible seaweed; how to fish from the ocean and off piers and eat raw fish; how to snorkel and scuba dive; how to cook with soy bean paste and how to enjoy the freshest produce from the local vendors at the farmers markets. I rented a cottage amongst former plantation workers. My screenplay, "Sweet Dusty Road," derives from the times I was neighbors with these loyal, hard-working people.

I welcome the opportunity to tell the world that there is a place in the sun for anyone thirsting for real people who perpetuate love. I've enjoyed the fulfillment of nature, the serenity of the ocean, awesome sunrises and sunsets and most of all, the angels of aloha who occupy the island of Kauai. Every day there's reason to say, "I am so blessed!"

Growing Up On Kauai

Sugar Plantation Days

For 150 years, sugar plantations were an integral part of Kauai life, until the last sugar was harvested in 2009. Looking around Kauai now, you can imagine what the island looked like with tens of thousands of acres of bright green sugar cane fronds waving gently in the wind. You can almost hear trucks, known to locals as "haul cane" trucks, still rumbling down the highway, bringing their cargo of newly harvested stalks of cane from the fields to the mill for processing, loose pieces falling through the heavy chain truck carriages, only to be crushed on the road by other vehicles, a faint sweet smell filling the air.

Beginning in the mid-1800s, more than 400,000 immigrant laborers came to Hawaii to work on sugar plantations for opportunity and adventure. Workers, almost entirely men, came from China, Japan, Portugal, Puerto Rico, Korea, Spain, Germany and the Philippines. Brave souls willing to start new lives on Kauai endured long, grueling ocean voyages packed shoulder-to-shoulder like so much cargo.

When they arrived, they were assigned to various sugar plantations and provided housing in "camps," many of which were named for the ethnic group originally housed there, such as Spanish Camp or Korean Camp; for the town in which they were located, such as Koloa Camp; or for the plantation owner, such as Rice Camp, named for William Hyde Rice. As waves of laborers came and went, some returning to their home countries, camps retained their names long after their original population had moved on. Many families remained in the camps for years, descendants living in the same homes as earlier generations.

In addition to housing, most plantations also provided basic furniture, stoves, electricity and medical care for free to their employees.

Some say sugar plantation workers were segregated by ethnic groups for convenience and comfort, enabling them to live with others from their home country with whom they shared the same language and culture. Others say that plantation owners purposely separated ethnic groups from each other so they could not organize and request higher wages or better living conditions. Opinions on this topic vary as widely as workers' own experiences working for the plantations, ranging from short-term employment to careers that spanned decades until retirement.

Here are some stories of childhoods spent in sugar plantation camps and other memories of growing up on the Garden Island.

A "cane haul" truck laden with harvested sugar cane.
(Photo courtesy Grove Farm)

Growing Up in a Plantation Camp
By Niles Kageyama

Niles Kageyama grew up in Japanese Camp in Koloa on the south shore of Kauai, the town where the first successful sugar plantation in Hawaii was founded. As a third generation Kauaian whose grandparents immigrated to Kauai from Okinawa and Japan, Niles forsook plantation work, as did many of his peers, heeding his calling to attend college to become a pastor.

Now retired from Koloa Missionary Church where he served as pastor for 19 years, Niles and his wife Aileen teach ukulele to elementary school students at Koloa School, the same school Niles attended as a boy. Niles recalls his colorful childhood growing up in a sugar plantation camp.

I grew up in Japanese Camp in Koloa, located behind where First Hawaiian Bank is now. Next to us was Filipino Camp, and where the bypass road is now was Portuguese Camp. There was also Spanish Camp, but by the time I was growing up, most of the people living there were Filipinos. The original Spanish who came to work in the plantations had all returned home after serving out their contract terms.

Growing up in a plantation camp, everybody knew each other. We knew who was sick, who got into trouble, who was having a baby and so forth. Everybody helped one another.

Fun and Games

As children growing up in plantation camps, we didn't know we were poor. We made our own games and came up with our own toys. We were never bored. We used to play Fight Sword with swords made from panax plant stalks. We'd find one that was kind of straight and peel it. If you want to be "someone" you picked a bigger one, but the bigger ones were slower so most of us chose the smaller ones. All the adults would say, "Danger! Danger! No play that game! You poke somebody's eye!" But we had a rule to hit only below the waist.

Did you play Five Hole Marbles when you were a kid? If you didn't, you were so deprived! We would dig five holes in the ground and try to get our marbles into those holes. How about the game called "Alabia?" We stuffed Bull Durham tobacco pouches with leaves from the panax hedges and threw them at each other. Before we started we decided whether the alabia was going to be soft, medium or hard and we would check each other's alabia to make sure both sides had the same type. We played these games for hours.

We did a lot of other outdoor things like swimming in the ocean and the reservoir. I learned bass fishing at Waita Reservoir. I used dojo for bait, a little slimy eel-looking fish. It was very hardy. You could hook it and it would be alive for hours. I must have spent half of my childhood climbing trees through mango, lychee and guava seasons. It's a wonder that I cannot remember anyone ever falling down and breaking anything. I still climb trees, by the way, but my wife gets after me.

We used to go camping with multiple families. We'd be in someone's boathouse and talk story, and run on the sand dunes at Mahaulepu. We'd find old Hawaiian bones. I remember one day the guys went hunting and they found this skull. One guy put the skull on a stick and all the adults shouted, "Aaaah, put it back!"

Sometimes we would get our pocket knives and sit down in the fields and cut sugar cane and chew until you could not chew anymore. One of the great joys of life.

It wasn't all fun and games. We did attend Koloa School. Many of us attended church. One was called the brown church, the other was called the white church, because one was painted brown and the other was painted white. The brown church was an independent Hawaiian church where missionaries ministered. They came and talked to us when we were young, in about the third grade. We ended up with a lot of Japanese in this Hawaiian church. It was there I received my calling from the Lord when I was 16.

Picture Brides

My story and my wife's story are kind of typical of what happened to the immigrant workers who came to Kauai from Japan and Okinawa and how their lives ensued. My grandparents immigrated to Kauai from Japan and Okinawa; I'm half Japanese and half Okinawan.

Most of the immigrants who came from Japan were single men. They heard that Hawaii was the land of golden opportunity. They planned to make their fortunes, send back a lot of money to Japan, then one day they would all retire in luxury in Japan.

That didn't pan out. That's why more than 50 percent of them returned to Japan before long. The rest decided it might not be better where they came from so they decided to stay in Hawaii. I'm really glad my grandparents didn't decide to return or I wouldn't be here today.

The Japanese men who decided to stay said, "I'm going to be here a long time and I need to start thinking about raising a family. There's a problem here. There are no Japanese women around so what are we going to do?"

This is where the picture brides came in. Japanese men in Hawaii would send their photos to Japan where a marriage would be arranged, then the women sent their photos back to Hawaii to their future husbands. Did this really happen? You better believe it. A lot of them!

When the picture brides arrived in Hawaii and disembarked after their long ocean voyage, the husbands would meet them, show their papers, then the couple could go straight to the immigration office on the dock where there was a justice of the peace waiting to marry them right then and there. If you didn't do that right away, some of the men would steal brides — maybe those who didn't have money to get their own!

Sometimes the man would send a picture of himself taken when he was much younger. That was a problem when the young bride arrived. When she got to Hawaii and met him, she would just cry and cry, but I don't think that was the norm.

My wife's maternal grandparents had an arranged picture bride marriage. One day when we were visiting them in Lawai on Kauai, my wife's grandmother showed us the very same photograph she had sent to her future husband when she was a picture bride.

My maternal grandparents, who came from Okinawa, were married in the immigration office right on the dock in Honolulu. I don't know if my grandmother was a picture bride, but I do know it was an arranged marriage.

What is so amazing is that very few of these marriages ended up in divorce.

My paternal grandfather came to Hawaii as an entertainer who would travel throughout the islands to the various sugar plantation camps. He would sing stories in a traditional Japanese narrative style of song called naniwa-bushi. After a hard day of work, the men would sit back after dinner and relax and my grandfather would sing to them. My dad told me my grandfather would sometimes be away from home, traveling six months to two years at a time.

One night when my grandfather was on stage, my grandmother was in the audience and she fell in love with him. In those days, entertainers were looked down upon and my grandmother's family did not approve of the relationship. When they decided to get married, her side of the family disowned her. When I was growing up, I never knew anything about that side of the family. Only many years later, I found out I had relatives on Kauai I never knew about.

It All Began with the Sugar Industry

My dad worked for the sugar plantation all his life. He was also very involved in the labor movement and was a very powerful union leader. He was actually revered by the Filipino laborers because he fought so hard for all workers in Hawaii. My father's name was Mac. My brother tells me that one time in Filipino Camp, residents there recognized him as our father's son. As he walked by, friendly voices shouted out to my brother, "Small Mac! Small Mac!"

My father's philosophy was, "Anything for better conditions." He constantly had union meetings. I went with him to various towns where we'd find the town hall and invite laborers. The most dramatic part was the strikes, mostly for higher wages. During strikes, fishermen and pig hunters would help set up community kitchens.

In the end it backfired against them as costs rose too high and plantations closed their doors. The Hawaii sugar cane laborers became the highest paid in the world. The industry in Hawaii could not compete with the foreign market, which paid minimal wages. I'm really glad that my dad died before the closing of the Koloa sugar mill. It would have broken his heart because he worked so hard for the laborers. It was needed at that time.

When the Koloa sugar mill closed down in 1996, it was the beginning of the end of an era. The last sugar plantation on Kauai shut down in 2009.

What did the sugar industry do for us? It provided a source of income for the first immigrants to raise a family. They didn't get rich as they thought they would. It provided a source of income for the second generation, which would be my parents, and they were able to send us to college. You wonder how in the world were they able to do that? But they did it. It gave many of us who were raised in a plantation town the experience of growing up in a close-knit community and a close family, willing to work hard and learning to be happy without a lot of things. And it gave us the unique experience of being raised in a multicultural environment, enriching our lives and helping us to relate to all kinds of people.

I think the sugar industry came to Hawaii at the right time, and it closed at the right time. It made Hawaii what it is today. Most of us would not be here if it wasn't for the sugar industry. I feel very privileged to have been born and raised on Kauai, being brought up in a plantation family, in a plantation camp, in a plantation town.

Rice Camp in the 1930s and 1940s

By Harry Yamanaka

Harry Yamanaka grew up in the 1930s and 1940s in Rice Camp, a settlement of small, wooden single-wall construction homes on dirt roads provided for employees by Kipu Plantation just southwest of Lihue. The privately-owned land of Kipu Kai is surrounded by the Hoary Head mountain range rising more than 2,000 feet, a pristine bay, and in those years, acres of sugar cane growing so tall it camouflaged the houses from outsiders. Harry was born the 10th of 13 children. His memories of growing up in Kipu bring the plantation camp alive again.

I can still see the old plantation house in Rice Camp where our family of 15 lived. It was a typical wooden, single-walled house that was made available to all plantation field workers with four bedrooms and one living room. The kitchen was separate, adjoined by a walkway. We all fit in the house somehow. We doubled up, slept on the floor. As a child I didn't think about it much because I didn't know any better.

Our neighbors on one side were Filipino bachelors who worked long hours and tended to their roosters tethered in the yard. Our neighbors on the other side were the Kagawas. I remember clearly Jimmy, one of the Kagawa sons, and his irritating whistle to signal the kids in our household to keep quiet.

The area around the camp was full of peacocks, roosters and hens. No one was allowed to catch them, and Kauai was free of mongoose, a natural predator, so the birds were everywhere. They slept in trees and woke up early to announce their delight at the new day. The crowing and cawing were incessantly present in the early morning hours. Did you ever hear the loud scream from a peacock or guinea hen in the darkness of early morning? It did not bother me but I am sure it would not be the same for someone who has never experienced this.

My father came to Kauai from Japan when he was 17. He became a trackman tending the plantation's railroad tracks. He also served as a middleman for the employees to talk about their problems and grievances to the management. He earned about $35 a month and that was more than many other men.

In those days, a penny went a long way. For instance, a loaf of unsliced bread cost five cents. School lunch cost five cents also. Schools did not offer free lunches for economically challenged families. Had there been such support, my family would have been highly qualified for that program.

Our life revolved around the small sphere of the plantation, Rice Camp, local fishing spots, Hamano Store and Seki Camp, which was another plantation camp nearby. We walked everywhere or we rode one of the two bicycles our family repaired and rebuilt, claimed after someone had thrown them away. When I visited Rice Camp several years after moving away, I jogged the three miles from Hamano Store to the main highway. I was surprised that this distance was such a short run, and yet at that time no one searched out this greater world.

Only two families in the camp owned cars and only one had a telephone that was shared by all the camp residents. No one else could afford such luxuries. If we were walking when a car came by, they almost always stopped to give you a ride. Back then, it was a joy to ride in a car.

*Harry Yamanaka with one of the two bicycles his family restored
after someone else discarded them, complete with a
Sears Roebuck seat cover. The bicycles were the family's
only modes of transportation other than walking.
(Photo, circa 1944, courtesy Harry Yamanaka)*

We shopped for necessities at Hamano Store, owned by a Chinese couple and managed by the husband. He usually gave you a piece of candy or ice cream or a soda if you made the trip to his store. Back then it was a very welcome item and everyone was thrilled to get it.

A person went door-to-door and took orders for rice and anything else you wanted from Hamano Store. The biggest item at that time was rice. It came in 100-pound bags. I worked part-time at Hamano Store as a stockman. As a teenager I could stack bag after bag after bag. It was a real struggle for people to take the rice bags home without cars, but the store had a pick-up truck that delivered them.

The wife of the Hamano store couple was a schoolteacher at Huleia School, and she was very, very good in teaching you the basics of English. Most of us were not totally immersed in proper English usage. We spoke Pidgin English and Japanese at home. She did a very good job because six of our eighth grade graduating class of 10 went to college and did very well. We Huleia School students still have reunions and we talk about the old times.

There was only one policeman in the area. His presence got everyone's attention. Actually there was no need for police work because most of the problems were handled internally and most were non-violent. None of the homes had keys to the door. Break-ins were non-existent. Besides, what was there to steal?

Fun and Food

We were always on the lookout for ways to bring home more food. My father often carried a sack of pumpkin and squash seeds that he planted along the irrigation ditches as he walked to work. A few months later, he would direct us to harvest those plants that had mature vegetables. It was fun looking for pumpkins and squash in the honohono *(wild orchids)* and buffalo grass.

My brother, Goro, was an expert maker of bamboo fishing poles that had a whip excellent for setting the hook on a fish. He started with a mature, long, sturdy stalk of bamboo, then he built a small fire and passed the nodes of the bamboo over the heat. The bamboo softened and became pliable. As sap oozed onto the surface, he wiped the oily beads with a rag. In a few minutes, an original green bamboo pole would be finished and leaned against a wall to dry for about two weeks.

As boys, we fished at reservoirs stocked with black bass called Charlie Fish. One reservoir, called Turning, had an abundance of fish but an oft-told story about the ghost of Felix scared a lot of us away. During my brothers' long walks to and from Huleia Valley to the east of Rice Camp, they brought back fish including papio, mullet, goby and aholehole, supplementing the small amount of meat our family could get. My older brother, Sam, was very good at catching Samoan crabs and he sold his catches to the villagers. It seemed that everyone in the family had a role to play in those times of plantation survival.

I helped by catching frogs. Frogs are very good eating, something like exquisite chicken. Cleaning frogs was easy. Just cut the head off, rip the skin from the neck down and take out the guts.

Frogs were plentiful in ditches. On some frog-catching expeditions with a neighbor, I caught a half bag or more. One day when visiting Hanalei with a friend, I learned that frogs were even more abundant and easier to catch in the taro fields on the island's north shore. We walked along the earthen dikes between the taro patches and instead of spearing them, my friend just put one leg in the water and caught them at the throat by jamming them against the dirt banks. I was the bag boy and in the end the gunny sack was almost full of live frogs. It got so heavy I had to say, "Enough!" My friend chopped off the legs from the trunk section and told me he sent them to a restaurant in Honolulu and made an excellent profit.

As an adult, I ordered frog legs in Paris, but the French always add a dressing to go with it. I prefer them with shoyu (soy) sauce.

Our family had three large vegetable gardens, supervised by our mother. I earned pocket money by selling burdock, a plant much in demand by Japanese families for use of the crunchy root called gobo in nishime, a traditional Japanese stew made with root vegetables. Gobo is difficult to grow because the dirt has to be softened about two feet from the top to provide a good media for growing long and tender roots. My father allowed me to keep the money from selling gobo to meet my various expenses. My bank was a small drawer where I kept loose change. In those days it was not wise to hold money in your pockets because of the bullies who took whatever you had.

We picked fresh fruit from trees growing in the area, including mountain apples, guava and green mangoes. Half-ripe mangoes were a favorite, especially when seasoned with shoyu and salt, or with sugar. During mango season we carried small packets of the spices in our pockets so we were ready whenever we came upon the delicious fruit.

To satisfy one's sweet tooth more, we walked along the train tracks that ran through the plantation and picked up stalks of fallen sugar cane. We sliced off the skin with a pocket knife and chewed the pulp to get to the sweet sugar. We also made arrows of the long leaves with our knives, whipping the leaves into the air and watching the arrows fly to distant spots.

Harry lived in Rice Camp until he was 18 years old, when he left to attend college in Milwaukee, working until midnight to fund tuition and pay for an apartment. After graduation, he served for three years in the U.S. Navy on a radio repair ship on which he traveled to Russia, Hong Kong, Guam and Singapore. He returned to Hawaii where he became a teacher and later became an administrator for the Department of Education. After retiring, Harry taught English in Japan.

I am now 83 years old and my life growing up at Kipu Plantation is only memories. The plantation is now a ranch, owned privately, and worked by only several men. An ATV tour company occupies former school grounds. Hamano Store is gone, as are other landmarks in the area.

When I last visited, Rice Camp was still there but the row of green houses where the Yamanaka house stood are gone and only cattle and wild pigs roam that piece of land. I can relive that life only in my dreams. But, then, what is life without dreams?

Yamanaka family circa 1936, from left, Kitt, Haruno (mother), Gladys, Juliet. Esther, Margie, Paul, Sam, Goro, William, Kichijiro (father), Harry (blurred). Three more kids were not yet born or too young to stand up for the photo: Edith, Doris and Jeanne. (Photo courtesy Harry Yamanaka)

Local Haole

Holbrook 'Hobey' Goodale

Holbrook "Hobey" Goodale's roots on Kauai stretch back generations. His great-great grandparents were among the first wave of missionaries to land on Kauai in 1820. His great-grandfather on his father's side was a printer who founded The Honolulu Advertiser newspaper in 1856 (merged into another paper in 2010), and was also the postmaster general of Hawaii, who printed the two-cent missionary postage stamps that are now highly prized by collectors.

Hobey's great-grandfather on his mother's side, William Hyde Rice, was fortunate enough to purchase 3,000 acres of land in Kipu Kai from Princess Ruth Keelikolani for $3,000 in 1872. There he operated Kipu Ranch, and when he was 26 years old, established Kipu Plantation.

Hobey was born in 1923. His childhood was a combination of privilege, hard work and boyhood pranks. Now retired as president of Garden Island Motors, a family-owned automobile dealership that was sold in the late 1990s, Hobey is a well-respected philanthropist, who loves to reminisce about his rascal days.

Local Haole

Our family was kind of ostracized by other haoles *(slang for Caucasians)* because my grandfather had changed from being a Republican to the Democratic party back in the mid-1930s. Other Caucasian families wouldn't have much to do with us so I didn't see myself as haole. I thought haoles were bad. I beat up on them every chance I got.

I had a lot of Japanese friends. I couldn't really speak Japanese, but I could use enough Japanese words to be understood. But if they were talking about me, thinking they were talking behind my back, I knew what they were saying. But I never let on.

Once my grandfather put me and a Japanese boy about 18 years old together as a team to dig fencepost holes on the ranch. These older Japanese men were just beating the Hell out of us boys, making more fencepost holes than we could, and faster, until we got the knack.

One day one Japanese man said to me, "Hey, Mistah Hobey, you good, hard worker. What you need is a good Japanese wife." He said he'd be my matchmaker. In those days nobody married across boundaries. East was east and west was west, and nary the two shall meet. But I took his offer as a compliment.

One afternoon during World War II, some of my co-workers and I were told to search the houses of some Japanese people we worked with. The government was worried they were going to harm the country when we were at war with Japan. Here's the guy you sit down and have lunch with and now you've got to go search his house? Kind of hard. We didn't search so good. We didn't give a damn.

During World War II, when soldiers were stationed on Kauai, I was concerned I'd get blamed if any young woman I'd spent time with, turned up pregnant by a soldier. I kept myself busy and out of trouble — by gambling! Down at Nawiliwili I played the Filipino game of paiute, craps and pool. I would gamble with anyone who came along. I'd watch them play pool for awhile, then I'd say, "I think I can take this guy." I made quite a bit of money at dice and cards, so when I finally met Nancy *(his wife of 60 years who passed on in 2008)* and got engaged, I could buy the ring.

The first time I attended a cockfight, the Filipinos were really upset. They said, "Oh, boss's grandson. No good." One of the Japanese cowboys told them, "Oh, no worry for him." I was betting on somebody's chicken. We had a great time.

The way the road was, the police had to come across a bridge and around in a big circle to get to where the chicken fights were. Just below the chicken fights in the bamboo was a place where two guys hid, playing cards while keeping an eye out for police cars. When they'd see one, they would yell, "Umayen!" (*Coming!*). Everyone would grab the chickens and go out in the brush and hide until the cops were gone. It was very seldom that the police caught anyone.

Before there were stoplights on Kauai, we had a traffic director, a guy in a 50-gallon barrel-like thing that was made out of canvas. He had a sign atop that said "Stop" or "Go." He sat in the barrel and directed traffic, near where Bank of Hawaii is on Rice Street in Lihue now. He would blow a whistle: "Brweeet!" People obeyed him.

The Depression and Okolehao

I was 10 years old when the Great Depression started in 1933. We had an easy life because we had a dairy, we had milk and cream. My grandfather got a couple Guernsey cows and a Guernsey bull. We'd make 10 to 12 pounds of butter a week. We had our own churn. We also had a vegetable garden. We had ducks and chickens, so we had eggs. If we slaughtered the cattle, we could get beef.

The Okinawan family farmers had a hard time. They built a cannery named Hawaiian Fruit Packers, mauka *(toward the mountains)* on Kawaihau Road in Kapaa, but they couldn't sell their product and one by one they went broke. So we'd pull into the fields and load up the back of our touring car full of pineapples. Then we'd go home and make pineapple crunch and pineapple preserves.

People found ways to make money any way they could during the depression. One day my stepfather was riding his horse along the forest reserve fence when he came upon a Chinese man who had an illegal still where he was making okolehao, Hawaiian moonshine made from the root of ti plants. My grandfather said, "I don't see nothing. But you know where I live, eh?"

In about two weeks comes a five-gallon barrel of White Oak. They called it White Oak because to mellow out all the rotten stuff in the okolehao they aged it in five- and 10-gallon oak barrels. When the man brought it to the house, my stepfather wasn't home. Mother went out and said to the man, "You bring for Mister, but what about Missy?" He must have kept the barrels coming because years later, we found about 65 gallons of okolehao in the closet under the big double-staircase that led upstairs.

Rascal Days, Surfing & Sugar Cane

In those days outhouses were built over plantation irrigation ditches. Boys balled up newspapers and set them on fire, then sent them floating down the ditches. Folks got their backsides singed while doing their business. I wasn't part of that. I was a good boy.

I liked taking the stingers off centipedes. I'd choose the big ones, like seven inches or more. I would cut out the two front stingers with a knife. Then I'd put a centipede on my head under my hat, where it would curl up and sleep because it was dark and warm. I'd go down after work to Lihue Store, see my aunt or friend of my grandmother. I'd say, "How do you do?" and tip my hat. They would see the centipede and scream!

Our house was right on the beach at Kalapaki. We got surfboards and we didn't know how to surf. We really were trying to kill ourselves! Sam Kahanamoku *(brother of Hawaiian surfing legend and Olympic swimming champion Duke Kahanamoku)* came and got in the water with us and showed us how. I took to it right away.

Our surfboards were solid wood so going out was easy but coming back they would be waterlogged and heavy. Mine was about 10 feet long and I also had a couple of smaller ones. We'd lean them up against the side of buildings to drain out.

I enjoyed surfing big waves. The bigger the better. But I didn't think about it. Years later, a friend told me, "Hobey, you and one of your friends used to go out in the biggest waves where nobody else would go." I loved getting out in the water and challenging the waves. I surfed mostly with Hawaiian and Japanese boys at Nawiliwili. In those days you didn't have a car and when the war came along you only got three gallons of gas, so you didn't go far. We just surfed down at Nawiliwili, or if there was no surf, we would go diving, spear fishing.

Every afternoon we'd walk up the hill at Kalapaki Bay, opposite where the houses are now. As kids we walked everywhere, and we were barefoot all the time. We'd just walk through a patch of hilahila *(a thorny weed)*, like there was nothing to it. We had tough, tough feet.

Usually the sugar cane that was planted above Kalapaki was a relatively soft cane so it was good. We would go up in the cane field, break off a long branch but we'd only take the bottom, the old part, where the sugar had been sitting for awhile, then come back and chew cane and watch for fish in the bay. We'd peel the cane and then gnaw on it. I don't know how we had teeth left. I had a good time.

Holbrook "Hobey" Goodale at his home in Lihue.
(Photo by Pamela Varma Brown)

Pidgin English

An endearing and enduring contribution from the early days of the sugar industry in Hawaii is the creation of Pidgin English, a verbal shorthand blended from English, Hawaiian, Chinese, Japanese, Filipino, Portuguese, Spanish and other languages, enabling people of a myriad of nationalities to communicate with each other.

Spoken with a distinct accent and lilt, Pidgin follows no formal rules other than to get a point across in the most economical use of words. Verbs are often ignored and almost everything is spoken in present tense. Context, including gestures and surroundings, often provides as much explanation as the words themselves.

Pidgin English quickly became an essential part of communication among sugar, and eventually pineapple plantation employees, and is still widely spoken throughout the islands in informal settings. Here's a sampling of Pidgin English you might hear on Kauai.

Standard English: I will be with you in a moment.
Pidgin English: Try wait.

Standard English: If you can do it, please do so. But if you cannot, I understand.
Pidgin English: : If can, can. If no can, no can.

Standard English: You are doing that exactly the way I taught you.
Pidgin English: That's the how!

"Da kine" is a multi-purpose phrase that can be used when the exact name of an item or person doesn't come to mind; it also means "great," or "wonderful," or almost anything else you need it to mean in the moment.

Standard English: Please hand me that item on the table.
Pidgin English: *(Pointing)* I like da kine.

Standard English: We are out of stock of the product you are asking for.
Pidgin English: No mo' da kine.

Standard English: This is better.
Pidgin English: Mo' bettah.

Best lease negotiation:
Lessee: "Are you going to give me a lease for this office space I am renting from you?"
Lessor: "No need. You pay, you stay. You no pay, you go."

Common Pidgin English words and phrases:
Pau hana — after work; done with work
Ono grinds — delicious food
Chicken skin — goose bumps
Talk story — chat
No need — no need

Plantation-Style
Alfred Ringor

Alfred Ringor grew up in Puhi Camp, a community of approximately 600 homes built in the 1920s by Grove Farm Company, where his father worked on the sugar plantation as a "cane haul" truck driver. "In those days, Kauai was all cane," he recalls. Now an auto mechanic, Alfred helps maintain Hawaiian Telcom's fleet of vehicles and is also an automotive instructor at Kauai Community College, located where Puhi Camp once sat.

Sprinkling Filipino words and Pidgin English seamlessly into his sentences, blending present and past tense as is customary in Pidgin, Alfred recalls with laughter and wistful smiles days gone by growing up plantation-style in the 1960s and 1970s on Kauai.

I remember growing up in old Puhi Camp. Everything was provided: a place to play, trees to climb. We played in the irrigation ditches, climbed mango trees. We enjoyed it.

Puhi Camp always felt safe because everybody knew us. Every place we would go in the camp people knew who we belonged to, so no can make any kine (*mischief*). The neighbors, they no scared to scold us if we do something wrong. They'll scold you as if you belong to them. We respected that.

We lived in the Filipino section of the camp. Up the hill had Japanese. On the other side was Portuguese. You could tell because the Portuguese side was really clean and neat. The Japanese had really nice gardens, orchids. Filipinos, if cannot eat 'em, they not going to plant 'em. So whatever had fruits li' dat *(like that),* they planted.

The Malunggay tree, every Filipino house had one. We call 'em Filipino flagpole. Everybody say it like Kalamungai, maybe because Pidgin. The fruit is long, looks like one drumstick. You boil it with soup and it tastes good. I remember eating that soup. It was so good it would drip down your elbow.

The plantation housing I remember had two steps that went up, a small little gate and a small little porch. When you walk in, get one big living room. One big bedroom, so we'd all sleep in there. Plantation houses had iron roof. It's loud when it rains! You sleep good when it rains hard.

The washroom was detached. Never get flushing toilets, had like an outhouse. Before we sat down, we had to roll up pages from the thick Sears catalogs, burn them and swirl them around to get rid of crawlers, insects that had crawled up on the seats.

When I was about 11 years old, we moved right up the road. That was an upgrade because we had flushing toilets. That was different! I couldn't really adapt to it, because I was so used to the outside. That house had been one of the plantation boss's. It had three bedrooms, a bathtub, and lychee and mango trees in the yard.

Every Sunday one house near our new home would have a lot of cars parked around. I thought it was a church. But it was chicken fights. We walked up there one day and we saw all the chickens in the ditch and guys were playing cards and gambling. My dad no used to gamble or chicken fight. He no like giving money away. For leisure he went bowling.

Had a lot of single guys working for the plantation and we had nicknames for every one of them. One was "Bike Man" because when we parked our bikes, he'd take them away and hide them inside the cane field. We never did get them back.

Frog Frisbees

After school we would play outside until dark. Whenever we used to play kickball in the dirt road, we'd use flattened frogs as the bases. Had so much toads that whenever we'd come home, we'd see the heads sticking up on the roads. Every time we would ram at least three or five of them. Cannot avoid them. Couple days later, they'd be so flat because people would run over them so many times. It's so dry, that thing. We'd just grab 'em and sling 'em like a flying saucer, like Frisbees. They'd go pretty far.

We also used our slippers (*rubber thong sandals*) for bases. We would run around barefoot with all the gravel and all that. We'd play outside so much in our slippers, we would have a V on our feet where we were sunburned from the strap. That would stay with us the longest time.

We would also play slingshot. We'd look for guava trees to make the Y. We'd sling rocks. There was so much on the dirt road, we never ran out of rocks. We'd shoot at yellow-jackets (*wasps*), the big nests on the old houses underneath the eaves, then run away so fast.

We'd catch guppies and fighting fish, the swordtails, in irrigation ditches. We'd bring 'em home, raise 'em, make 'em fight. They'd really fight with each other. The ones who lost, we'd find them floating.

When it was time to go home, had to wash our feet in the banyo (*Tagalog for bathroom*). All the banyos had a ditch that ran downhill.

Our house was below everyone else. Their stuff would wash down past our banyo. Sometimes we would go uphill, make paper boats and float them down to the next house.

Sharing Food

My dad had a 1957 Chevy. For our family time, we would all get in the car and we all would sit in the same seats each time. I would sit behind the driver seat because I'd think that's where a man sits, and I could see how to drive and where we were going. We would go in that Chevy to pick fruits and vegetables on the back roads.

Being that my dad worked on the plantation, he knew all the fields and knew exactly where get all the vegetables, and where we can harvest. Those things were growing wild. We'd get squash and lilikoi (*passion fruit*). Right on top the hill of the irrigation ditches, alongside the cane, bitter melon vines would be growing. Bitter melon is a delicacy for Filipino food. We would cook it in soup and mix it with chicken.

We would load up that truck and leave the rest for the next person. The next family would be driving up as we were driving away. We would share whatever we cooked with our neighbors. The neighbors, they all come and bring whatever they cooked.

Every time my dad would go to work, he would check the small white announcement board for community get-togethers. That's when all the Portuguese, all the Japanese, all the Filipinos would come and get together because they all had something in common. They all worked for the plantation. There was good camaraderie among the parents. The children, we would all fight, pick on each other, but in front of our families, we gotta act good so we don't get scolding.

Around the Clock

My grandfather worked for Gay & Robinson Sugar Plantation. My dad was a truck driver for the Grove Farm Plantation. When Lihue Plantation bought the place, he transferred.

In those days, plantations were the main opportunity for work. They had plumbers, electricians, carpenters, truck drivers, engineers. They had everything. Working in hotels was the other option. I ended up in a hotel, working at Coco Palms.

Plantation work was around the clock: harvesting, planting, mills running. Dad used to have the 2 to 10:30 p.m. shift. Sometimes he worked all night and got off work in the morning. Some mornings before he came home he would stop at Ma's Restaurant for breakfast. We used to meet him. Other plantation workers would be there, too. He'd still have all his dirty clothes on. I remember his neck was all red from the red dirt. When he'd get home, he'd take a shower but you could still smell that cane field smell. Maybe that's what made me go into hotel work, that cane field smell.

Just before harvest, sugar plantations burned fields of cane to dispose of unusable green leaves, so that only stalks of cane remained to be trucked to the mills for processing. On "burn days," dark smoke billowed in the trade winds, filling the sky.

They used to send us letters saying they were going to burn cane. So if we had laundry drying outside on burn days, we'd take it in. Ashes would fly; they would float all around the place. We'd have to sweep the patio.

When they burned at night, it was exciting. We'd go to the edge of the field where they would have all the trucks and lots of lights set up. It would be like a mini-carnival, a small little circus. The fire glowed bright orange. My dad used to tell us when they burned the cane, the wild pigs would run out and they'd shoot them. It was an easy hunt to bring home food.

In the late 1940s, Grove Farm built a narrow, half-mile tunnel through the mountain between Puhi and Koloa to reduce the time it took to transport cane to the processing mill. An engineering marvel, the tunnel is still standing with no supports and has no wiring for lights.

My dad used to sneak us on the cane trucks and ride us through the tunnel in the mountain to Koloa at night. We waited on the side of the road and he used to pick us up. In the tunnel at night, it was scary, so dark. All you see is one small little light at the end. I don't know how they used to know if someone was coming toward them. My dad used to tell me the drivers used to play jokes on each other by putting mannequins inside the tunnel to look like a real man. From far away it was frightening. You never know if it was real.

Riding in the big cane haul trucks was neat because you sit way up high. You get the road all to yourself on the back roads. My dad knew every single turn.

Shopping Plantation-Style

I liked the Mom and Pop stores, walking in and the people would just know you off the bat. I remember going into Puhi Store. We'd just grab candies off the shelf, put them on the counter. The guy would write it down on the charge paper and would just trust. Our folks would pay later on the next payday.

Yoneji Store at Rice and Kalena streets, that building is still there but the store is gone. They had so much stuff overflowing. The aisles were so small and the wagon just fit. They had small little shopping baskets. I don't know how we got all the stuff in our basket but we did. It seemed like they didn't take inventory. They'd just order stuff and just bring 'em in, everything just stacked up, nothing displayed. You'd say, "You get this?" They'd say, "Oh, maybe around the corner of that aisle."

At Kress Store they had colored popcorn, coated in red, green. They had 'em in the front window. The coating was all sugar.

The post offices had glass windows for the mailboxes so you could see if you have mail. That was all family kine, so if they see you have mail, they would just grab it and go running home and give you your mail. That was honesty, eh?

I've seen all these kinds of things disappearing. Plantation days are gone already. But I'm glad I experienced those times.

Growing up plantation-style taught me to get along with different cultures, eat different dishes, and just make do with what we get. I'm glad I can look back at plantation life.

Pineapple Days
By Ismael 'Pineapple Sam' Tabalno

Ismael "Pineapple Sam" Tabalno is a lively man with a quick wit and quicker smile, who grew up in Spanish Camp, a cluster of about 22 wooden houses in Koloa on Kauai's south side. By the time Sam's parents moved to Kauai in 1946, seeking opportunity after World War II decimated their home region of the Philippines, Spanish Camp residents were mostly Japanese, Chinese and Filipino, laborers in Kauai's rapidly growing sugar industry.

Sam shares stories of growing up the youngest of eight children in a camp house, the benefits of working in pineapple fields and the techniques he and his friends used as teenagers to meet girls vacationing on Kauai. After 40 years living on the mainland, Sam moved back home to Kauai in 2012.

The house we lived in when I was growing up in Spanish Camp was a testament to using what you had. It had 3 bedrooms, a living room, a kitchen and a front porch, all in about 800 square feet. When I was little, I slept on the floor of my parents' bedroom. When I was about 10, I moved to my brothers' room. Three boys in one bed! I was in the middle because I was the smallest one. Sometimes I would sleep with my head between their feet.

I think the hardest part for my parents about coming to Hawaii was leaving one of my brothers and one of my sisters behind in the

Philippines with our grandparents, but they were convinced that the opportunities here were better.

Most of my friends were right there in Spanish Camp. We didn't have those Nintendos and all the stuff they have today. We had sword fighting. We made swords out of bamboo sticks. We wanted to be Zorro. We played Cowboys & Indians, Hide & Seek, Bean Bag Toss and stuff like that. My friends were Japanese, Chinese, Filipino, Tonganese and one hapa-haole *(half-Caucasian)*. We called ourselves the "Spanish Camp Boys."

Growing up and meeting all these different people, Pidgin English was the only way you could talk with people of other cultures. Everybody took a little bit of their own language and that's how you were able to communicate, that's how we got closer.

The foods kind of mingled together, just like the language. We've got Korean kimchee, the Japanese daikon *(radish)*, and bagoong *(Filipino fermented fish)*. We learned how the same vegetable could be prepared differently.

It's sad to say, there were some biases that started in the camps. Some people would say, "Oh, never date Japanese girls because of this," or "Don't date haoles *(Caucasians)* because of that." But my mom was so against any of this prejudice. She taught me that people are not to be foolishly misjudged by their differences or appearance, but are to be valued for who they are. That gave me a foundation to be able to look at people not only seeing the color of their skin or the way they live. I easily got along with everyone.

Shoes & Sugar

I attended Koloa Elementary School for eight years. I went barefoot or wore slippers *(rubber sandals)* most of the time at school. We used shoes when we had a dance at school. Most of the time it was, "Shoes? What are you talking about?" We always kept our shorts on under our school clothes so when school was over we could go right to the beach or to play.

I went on many exciting escapades on the long trek to and from school. I explored man-sized storm drainage ditches that led to lava tunnels under the main road, scaled the oldest sugar plantation ruins in Hawaii, threw rocks at bullfrogs in the creeks, swam in shallow mountain spring water and other fun adventures. My mother used to ask me how in the world my clothes got so dirty just by attending school.

My father earned $100 per month as a sugar cane irrigator for Grove Farm Plantation, managing the flumes or irrigation ditches in various fields as he was assigned. He'd get up at 4 o'clock in the morning and he wouldn't come home until 4 o'clock in the afternoon. He worked for the plantation until he retired.

Back then, working for the plantation was the norm. People thought when we all were of age, everybody's going to work for the plantation, whether sugar or pineapple. When I was in high school, I was looking at which plantation I was going to work for. Did I want to be a planter or an irrigator? Until I got a little bit smart. After sampling the sugar cane fields, pineapple fields and then tourism, I favored tourism. When I was night manager for the Kauai Sands hotel, it was mo' bettah *(more better)*. I got to meet so many interesting people.

Pineapple Summers

When I was 15, 16 and 17, I worked in the pineapple fields during the summers on the 3 to 11 p.m. shift. That was ideal so we could hang out at the beach most of the day and work during the cooler evening. The pay was 50 cents per hour for the day shift and

55 cents for the evening shift. Not bad for the mid-1960s when gas averaged only 25 cents per gallon.

I enjoyed working in the pineapple fields more than in the sugar fields because I had more camaraderie with my co-workers. When I worked in the sugar cane fields, I was more isolated. I worked way back in the boonies and there was only one or two of us out there. Our job was to make sure that the ditches didn't get clogged up and that irrigation water kept flowing. We'd have to push the cane away from the roads and tend to the fields. It was not too entertaining. Whereas in the pineapple fields you get a group of 10 or 15 people for each 60-foot conveyor boom truck and you're all working together for one goal: to get the pineapple onto the truck. You had teamwork.

We wore lots of protective gear so we didn't get cut to shreds by the long, stiff, thorny pineapple leaves. I wore a long-sleeved shirt, red handkerchief scarf, jeans with canvas chaps, leather boots, gloves, clear plastic goggles and a wide brim straw hat.

When we first started, the old timers on our team showed us how to pick pineapples. You grasp a pineapple crown in each hand and push them away and down from you, and snap them off the plant. Then you bring them up, one pineapple in each hand, then twist and snap your wrist so the pineapple crown would separate from the pineapple, so only the fruit goes into the truck. We'd do this in one smooth, swift motion. Everybody had to grab one pineapple in each hand. That's the only way you could fill up the truck quickly. Each truck bin fully loaded held approximately 5,000 ripe or almost ripe pineapples. They are heavy and it is hard work. But you're young and you're strong, and you get a technique to it. I enjoyed it.

There was a friendly rivalry between the day shift and night shift. We young bucks, we knew that we could play around in the daytime. The people who worked the day shift usually had families. They came early in the mornings and by afternoon were home with their families. I think we night shifters could fill the truck faster. Sometimes we'd fill it up so fast that we had to wait for another empty truck to come back from the cannery.

After an eight-hour shift, most of us were exhausted, but as teenagers, some were still ready to party and meet up with new tourist girls we met during the day at the beach. We'd do this all summer.

I worked in the Kapaa Cannery when I was 16. We didn't have OSHA (*Occupational Safety and Health Administration, a government safety agency*). It was so noisy, and when you left the place you reeked of sweet pineapple juice all over your body. After awhile you got used to it.

My job was to make sure that the pieces of pineapple going to the juicer weren't wasted. I had a stick, kind of like a canoe paddle, and I'd walk down the aisle and make sure the channel didn't get clogged up. It was sort of boring because it was so noisy and I was the only one doing it.

Between the cannery and the field, I chose the field, because in the field you have the camaraderie, and you're outside in the open. You get a smell of pineapple but not as strong as in the cannery.

Pineapple Benefits

When we picked pineapples in sections of fields that were adjacent to the highway, occasionally cars and busloads of visitors stopped, waved at us and took pictures of our group vigorously picking pineapples. One time a tour group of about 20 girls on bicycles stopped to watch us. While we waited for an empty boom truck to replace the one we had just filled, our 10-minute break was enough time for many of us to hoot at the girls and find out where they were camping that night. They asked us to come visit them and told us to bring pineapples. About 10 of us met them that night.

When we went to the beach with our friends for fishing or other fun, we sometimes stopped along the fields and picked some pineapples for our day. Pineapple was easy food. It was fresh, it filled you up, gave you liquids you needed, and even though there were signs that said, "No trespassing. Do not pick," we thought, "Hey we're locals. We work here. We live here." If anyone tried to stop us they were probably our relative or friend. They'd say "Hey, what you doing? Let me show you where there are some better ones." We only picked enough to consume.

As an adult, I watch a lot of YouTube videos and I sometimes shake my head and wonder, "Who the heck taught you how to cut a pineapple?" I have posted three YouTube videos demonstrating how to cut a pineapple properly, most effectively. I post under my nickname, Pineapple Sam.

Tourist Girls & Dating

We'd meet tourist girls at the beach. Our opening line? We didn't have to say much. "Hey, what's up?" They were there to have fun, and we were fun people. If I met you back then, I'm sure you would have gone out with us. We were like magnets.

I worked at Hertz Rent-a-Car and my friends worked at a hotel. So when you arrived at Hertz Rent-a-Car, we knew where you were from, where you were going to stay, how many were in your party, everything. We would call our friend at the hotel and say, "So-and-so is going to be staying there." When we would meet you, we would know everything. We'd say, "Hey, you're from California." They'd ask, "How'd you know?" We'd say something like, "It's the way you walk."

Everybody wanted to try surfing, and of course I had friends at the surf hut. I'd tell the girls, "First of all, I don't think it's good to go body surfing with your bikini. You're going to have to take it off. I don't mean take it off now, you've got to put a one-piece on." We had girls who insisted, "No, my bikini's tight." As they came out of the water and they're pushing their hair back, their boobs are hanging out. They learned fast.

We also taught them how to sand slide. Take piece of plywood that we made in woodshop in high school and throw it over the sand when there's a sheen of water and you slide on it. We'd show the girls how to do it. We'd take girls hiking in the mountains; we'd go to the swimming holes and the beaches at the hotels.

Somebody once asked me, "Why do you always go out with haole (Caucasian) girls?" Well, when I dated local girls, a lot of them looked like my sister and my cousin and that felt kind of weird. Then after awhile I did date a few locals. Once I got into a martial arts duel with a guy behind Lihue Theater over a girl in high school. We went back there and duked it out. I won. Was the girl worth it? She told me she was finished with this guy, and I find out that they weren't. I finally said, "Bye."

Kauai only had a population of about 20,000 then and that made dating more complicated. You'd be dating this girl and she'd be the cousin of so-and-so and he'd say, "So when you going to get married?" I'd say, "What do you mean married? I'm just dating!"

Pineapple Sam

When I joined the Marines, they gave me the nickname "Pineapple." At first I kind of felt offended, because I wondered, "Are they making fun of me?" But then I realized, hey wait a minute, people like pineapples! It grew on me. I started using it and I like it. People say there's a ring to it.

I have written some books under my pen name Pineapple Sam about my Kauai and other life experiences. Some of the younger generation thinks I am just another uncle from Kauai. But when I tell stories, I watch their faces, their reactions, from the young ones to the older ones. I watch them smile and laugh and sometimes cry. I wanted to leave something behind, the legacy of Pineapple Sam, for my family, my relatives and all my friends on Kauai.

As a child, I knew Kauai was kind of special because why would all these people from all over the world come here to visit? I would ask them what it was like where they lived. From their descriptions, I started realizing Kauai is paradise.

How fortunate that I was able to grow up on Kauai! It was my beginning and now it's my end. After living away for 40 years, I am so happy to be back home on Kauai.

H. Wada Store

Aileen Kageyama

For more than 20 years, Aileen Kageyama's parents owned H. Wada Store, a general goods store near the pineapple cannery in Lawai, on Kauai's South Shore. It was one of the island's colorful and practical mom-and-pop stores.

Aileen, a music teacher at Koloa Elementary School, who with her husband, retired pastor Niles, also teaches ukulele to children after school, reminisces about her parents' store that launched three generations of Wada businesspeople on Kauai.

I was three years old when my parents opened H. Wada Store in 1946 in Lawai near what was then a pineapple cannery. We lived upstairs and the store was downstairs; the kitchen was in back.

You knew everybody who came in the store. And you knew everybody's business. I remember hiding a lady whose husband was chasing her with a knife. We hid her in the kitchen. It turned out OK, luckily. That was enough drama for me as a child.

In those days people lived in plantation camps arranged by their ethnic group. Customers would mingle with each other when they came into the store and talk to each other with their heavy accents in Pidgin English. That was our language.

We carried everything under the sun in that store. Food, household items, clothes. It was crowded inside. We didn't have a lot of refrigeration. The main refrigerator was for the soda pop and the freezer was for ice cream and popsicles. Our apples were displayed in the boxes they came in. We had all kinds of candies and treats, like what we used to call "crack seed," which are Chinese preserved plums. We had everything!

We sold a lot of Filipino food, like bagoong, made of fermented fish or shrimp, so we learned some Filipino words. We had Japanese food. We're Japanese so I was familiar with those foods. The foods for the different cultures were not as organized in the store as the people were in the plantation camps. They were kind of everywhere, but we knew where to find them.

In the summer the pineapple cannery operated day and night and we would service the workers. We brought in pastries from the local bakery; and if we ran out of food while cannery employees were working overtime, my mom would make up sandwiches in the kitchen and sell to them on their breaks. Occasionally, my mom would make cone sushi with the help of us children. These would sell like hotcakes. To our disappointment, there were never leftovers.

We Trusted Them

We would deliver for free. People could call in and we would write down their order. Of course, being children, we would groan, "Oh, we've got to put together an order." That meant we had to work, right?

When people placed an order, they would just say, "Charge it." We trusted them that they were going to pay. My dad worked in payroll at the cannery. On payday, he would say, "Come and get your change at our store after you pay your bill." My dad would show them what they got for their pay, then show them their bill for the store and give them their change. Wasn't that perfect?

It didn't matter what hours we set for the store. People still came by whenever they wanted something. My dad worked his usual hours at the cannery and then after work he would do the bookwork in the store and stay up as late as he needed to get it done. Even if they were closed, people came knocking on the back door. "Mr. Wada, I need to buy some bread." My father would say, "Come on in."

Every Wednesday we received three fresh items that people wanted and that we delivered: tofu, abura-age (*fried bean curd wrapper for cone sushi*), and konnyaku (*a traditional Japanese jelly-like health food made from a type of potato*). We received the tofu in 5-gallon cans. When we delivered, we would just walk into people's kitchens, put our hands in the can, lift out some tofu for them and put it into one of their bowls. Or we would get their bowl and bring it to the truck, fill it, then put it back their kitchens. They didn't have to be home. They knew it was tofu, abura-age and konnyaku day. Nobody locked their doors in those days. There was no need to.

When the cannery closed in 1965, I was away at college. A lot of people were losing their jobs. My father, who wasn't even 65 yet, and my mother said, "We might as well close the store."

They threw away a lot of what I would consider good things, like brand new overalls. We didn't have thrift stores then. They were probably overwhelmed and then had to move, too. I wish I had been here when they closed the store.

We had some land in Lawai for the longest time and my parents always talked about building a house there. We used to come and water the orange and lychee trees that my parents had planted. After they closed the store, my parents finally built their house and my grandparents moved into the house behind them. And now that my parents are passed on, my husband, Niles, and I live in the same house my parents built after they closed their store. I feel so fortunate. I had a very rich childhood.

Matsuura Store

By Shirley A. Matsuo

Shirley Matsuo and her husband moved to Kauai in 1975 to raise their two sons in a place where they could spend more time together as a family and enjoy the small-town feeling they had known while growing up on Oahu. When the family experienced the death of their husband/father, two hurricanes, high school graduation, countless ball games, potlucks and parties, Matsuura Store in Lawai was always there to help.

Matsuura Store, located next to the Lawai post office, was a remarkable part of the community. The owners were brothers Sakai and Masa Matsuura. Sakai, who was also the Lawai postmaster, was younger and serious-faced. Masa, a retired county worker was older, wore glasses, had gray hair and was chatty. Both brothers worked in the store daily. The store was open every day from 6 a.m. until 9 p.m., even on Christmas. The only day I remember they closed was when their mother died and they held a funeral.

Although the store looked disorganized, you could find almost anything you needed including bento lunches *(boxed lunches)*, drinks, pastries and snacks including their famous Lawai manju *(Japanese dessert of flour and red bean paste)*. You could buy school supplies, slippers *(rubber thong sandals)*, fishing gear, and once I even got a hair net there. If Sakai did well fishing, we could buy fresh fish. The brothers even provided personalized shelves where regular customers picked up their daily newspapers.

The brothers were kind and trusting enough to cash personal and other types of checks for regular customers. Of course there was no such thing as an ATM in those years. They even allowed known customers to charge their purchases if they were short on cash.

I have snapshots in my mind of the many times the Matsuura brothers helped my family in special ways. They provided snacks for my boys for the movies, tax-free. During a period when there was concern about pesticides in cow's milk, they made sure we all had safe milk to drink. After Hurricane Iwa destroyed our home, the brothers let us use their phone number so people could reach us. They provided bento lunches for my boys for school excursions when I couldn't get it together, and treats for the boys on Halloween. The brothers let us know that if my sons needed anything, they could use the store phone to call for help, and the store as a refuge if anything happened at the school bus stop.

They also gave us empty boxes for packing, beer boxes to carry dishes of food and cakes to potluck gatherings, and long sheets of white paper to use as last-minute table covers for parties. One Mother's Day, someone at the post office arranged for an anthurium corsage to be placed in my mailbox.

The Matsuura staff was the best: young students working after school and retired folks earning extra money who were pleasant and helpful. Sakai treated them like family. They ate meals and snacks there, and he financed trips to Las Vegas for some of them. Mark Oyama, now owner of the very popular Mark's Place and Contemporary Flavors Catering and a culinary instructor at Kauai Community College, worked at Matsuura store as a baker when he was a teenager.

The store served as an easy-to-find landmark where we could

meet people who came to visit us for the first time. It was also a hub of information. You could always learn about the latest happenings on Kauai at Matsuura store.

Time passes. The two brothers died and a third brother from Maui took over the store. The shelves for our daily newspapers were replaced by vending machines. In 1993, the third brother passed on and the store became a Menehune Mart, part of the Kauai-based Big Save Corporation, which was recently purchased by a larger grocery chain. The store still offers manju, bentos, sushi and pastry and the clerks are nice, but it is not the same.

I thank you, Matsuura brothers, for providing me with experiences and fond memories of a gentle, kinder time when people supported one another with daily, small but meaningful actions. Your caring created a feeling of security, ease and assurance that someone was there with the time and matter-of-fact attitude that the challenges of our daily lives could be overcome. I hope I continue to manifest this sense and have taught it to my sons.

The sign on the store is different now, but for me and old-timers of the west side of Kauai, we will always remember Sakai, Masa and Matsuura Store.

Hanapepe
By Shigeo Uyeda

Shigeo Uyeda was born in 1918 in Hanapepe, back when the now-sleepy town was a bustling center of activity. In 1986, when he was 68 years old, Shigeo's daughter asked him to write something about his life. He recalled snippets about growing up in Hanapepe, when the village had something for everybody.

Hanapepe was the center for the plantation workers east and west of it. Most of the businesses were family-owned by Chinese and Japanese, including a number of Chinese restaurants. I recall at school, instead of eating cafeteria food, running down the trail and buying piping hot bread generously spread with butter and jelly for five cents or manapua *(meat-filled or bean paste-filled buns)* for five cents, too. I guess my weakness for Chinese food started then.

When I first went to school, coming from a sugar plantation camp with only Japanese, a few Filipinos and a number of Chinese bachelors, I noticed for the first time Chinese boys and girls. Some of the girls seemed very attractive and different to this six-year-old Japanese boy. Many had English names like Hazel, Mildred, Amy, Florence, Grace and so forth.

Many of the boys had nicknames like Slim, Blackie, Whitey, Bunny, Sally and Stunt, and funnier ones, Pork and Beans, Meatball and Soup Bone. Since a lot of the haole *(slang for Caucasian)* teachers suggested the boys use English names so that the tutors didn't stumble, many selected new names. I remember my mother suggested adding Benjamin as my middle name because my uncle in Fresno was called Ben. It sounded good, but I didn't want to be burdened with such a long middle name for the rest of my life. Thus no middle name for me.

During our school years at Eleele School, from the edge of the campus you could see rice growing below and it was a beautiful and interesting sight to see, especially before harvest. Several crops were grown per year. I remember the high stands with strings radiating 360 degrees to the outer boundaries of the rice fields. Along the strings farmers hung rags and cans. Farmers tugged at the strings and a loud rattling sound chased away the pesty rice birds. When the tugging did not scare the birds, farmers fired short gun blasts.

Living in the camps, we used to walk a mile to the mill movie hall and always enjoyed seeing the shooting stars streaking across the heavens when returning late at night. We went to silent movies, mostly westerns such as Tom Mix, Yakima Canutt, Hoot Gibson and my favorite, Buck Jones.

Before electricity was strung to homes, Japanese movies came to the camps. They drove a car with a generator mounted on it to light the hand-cranked projectors. A person called a benshi would speak the male and female roles. I enjoyed the Japanese movies, especially the samurai pictures.

When silent movies became talking pictures, two movie theaters sprung up in Hanapepe, The Jardin Theater in 1931 and the Aloha Theater later, and Hanapepe became flooded with people during the multiple showings. I recall always coming out of matinees with a splitting headache. Today both theaters are closed.

In Hanapepe, we had two photo studios: Takasawa and Moscoso

Studios. Mr. Takasawa took the longest time getting ready and he had one of the cameras that rotated from left to right. I remember running from left to right with friends so our faces would appear twice on the same group picture.

At the Toyofuku Sweet Shop we were able to exchange one egg for a cone of ice cream. Then there was the old Chinese man with the wooden pole carrying two cans full of newspaper-wrapped roasted peanuts. He used to call softly, "Pea Nucky."

One of my classmates lived in Hanapepe Valley, in an area we used to call Minaha. When we picked fruit, we packed it in cans stuffed with leaves to prevent bruising, and floated them down an irrigation ditch. When we reached his home the cans were waiting, bobbing against the grate, where the flow into the siphon brought them across the valley for us.

As a child I remember watching my dad practicing horse racing and sulky (*two-wheeled horse-pulled cart*) racing at Hanapepe Stadium. The big race was held at Wailua on the east side of the island, where a lot of wagering took place. Track meets for youths were held regularly. I was never good in any sport, but I remember one race. As usual I was trailing far behind the first four clustered ahead of us when the first unfortunately stumbled, making the others fall on him, and I finished first.

There was a fisherman's village and fisherman's fleet near the Hanapepe River mouth. Fishermen's wives carried akule (*bigeye scad*) on wooden poles strung with morning glory vines and hau bark strips, selling for 25 cents a bunch. Later came fish peddlers in Model T Ford trucks with fly-proofed screened boxes. The peddlers had plum tree branches to swoosh away the flies while waiting for the customer to decide what cut and size she wanted.

150 Proof

Okolehao was the Hawaiian liquor made from the ti root. When the root and plant cooked, glucose formed. This sugar was fermented and distilled. Dad had a gleaming copper distiller and used it once or twice. A number of families financed their children's college education by bootlegging. Revenuers came infrequently, but when they did, the message spread fast and I recall only one family being arrested for illegal booze. My earliest recollection was Grandmother pouring okolehao from six bottles, a little from each, and filling the seventh, replacing the void in the first six with water. I am sure whomever drank the diluted stuff wouldn't know the difference because it was 150 proof or thereabout.

Dad made home-brewed beer and my maternal grandmother made sake (*Japanese rice wine*). I recall helping bottle the raw beer by adding a spoonful of sugar and capping. Bottles were stored away in the quiet for a few days until the frothy stuff was ready. Stores carried molasses, hops, caps and capping tools. Every home had the familiar earthen crocks to brew the stuff.

Ice was sold in blocks delivered by the McBryde Store truck until about the mid-1930s. It came in 100-pound blocks and was split into 25- or 50-pound pieces for the customers with an ice pick. Ice was kept in a homemade box with a top-opening lid, and the affluent homes had store-bought oak wood cabinets with the ice compartment on top and several compartments below. As kids, we used to follow the truck, gathering the small pieces of ice to play with.

Also in the mid-1930s, roller skating was a big fad. Hanapepe had three skating rinks. One is where the present post office is and another was where Lappert's Ice Cream is manufactured.

It was about 1929 when all the homes were wired for electricity.

Each plantation had its own generating system and supplied power for their respective camps and adjoining towns. Towns that had no plantation electricity source had their own electric company. Kapaa Electric and Waimea Electric were the town utility systems. Later, the east had Waiahi Electric, owned by Lihue Plantation. Eventually Waiahi Electric combined with the Kauai Electric Company.

At one time, the small airfield in Hanapepe was the airport for Kauai. I flew on light Cessna planes many, many times from there in my work to make periodic observations of the 10,000 sugar cane acres of McBryde Sugar Co. Early in World War II, I brought my Model T Ford, as did many others, to sit on the airport runway to prevent enemy landings.

The late U.S. Senator Spark Matsunaga, who served in the government for 27 years, grew up in Hanapepe. He was called "Sparky" because he was a good boxer with slow effective blows. Anyone who moved slowly was dubbed "spark plug" like the famous horse in the comic strip "Barney Google." I remember Matsunaga could not afford to go to college after high school so he worked for awhile as salesman for the Mikado Store. During his off hours he would go around soliciting subscriptions to The Garden Island newspaper with the sales pitch, "With your help I am going to college, and will devote my life to the people." I don't know whether my mother got the subscription, but I have voted for him whenever his name was on the ballot. He served from 1963 to 1990.

The Old Man Was Me

I have been an ardent gardener all my life. In the old days, we could tell who lived in the houses by what plants grew in their yards. Grapes were Portuguese, coffee and pigeon peas were Puerto Rican, malunggay were Filipino. Longan and lychee were Chinese, and Hawaiians had ti leaf plants. You know, I have all of the plants in my yard, so what am I?

I go swimming at Salt Pond Beach in Hanapepe every day. Along with me, "Uncle Louis" Almadova, Jr. is at the beach almost every day. He talks to as many beach goers, locals or visitors, as he can, and tourists return to Kauai because of Louis. He not only greets them, but carries a broomstick with a steel pick attached to the bottom. As he moves around, he spears rubbish and throws it away. He takes care of the lawn sprinklers by moving them from place to place. Together we have helped a number of innocent visitors who have gotten their vehicles stuck in the salt flats, and to recover car keys locked in car trunks.

Adjoining the beach is the salt pond area, where Hawaiians make salt in shallow flat pans. The salt is milder than the regular store-bought stuff. We loved broiled steaks smothered with this salt.

About 10 years ago I had the shock of my life at Salt Pond. Two Portuguese lads about 8 or 9 years old were racing each other. One yelled to the other, "Junior, that's the old man I was telling you about."

I looked around, saw nobody fitting that description, and suddenly realized the old man was me.

Innocent Times

Wilfred Ibara

Wilfred Ibara grew up on Kauai in the 1950s and 1960s when Waimea was a sugar plantation town. It was a simpler time for children, full of innocent fun. Now 70, with a sparkle in his eyes, a sweet, relaxed West Kauai disposition, and in a voice as flowing as the warm island breeze, Wilfred reminisces about some of his favorite memories growing up on Kauai and his youthful mischievousness.

I was brought up in a Waimea Mill Camp plantation house. It's still in existence, the last house on the highway in Waimea on the makai (*ocean*) side before the Waimea Plantation Cottages resort.

The first time I wore shoes was when I went to high school. Before that I never had shoes. We all went barefoot. Your feet used to get tough, really tough, almost like leather. I could run on hard pavement, walk on gravel. Today I cannot do that. In high school we wore regular covered lace shoes. It was a law. Even back then there were trends. The trend was to wear Bulldogs. The front was really massive, a boot front, almost like military shoes. That's what all the guys bought, Bulldogs.

When I was young, we played in the cane fields or played in the irrigation ditches or we'd go down to the beach and swim. Not like scuba diving, nobody could afford things like that. Nobody could afford a surfboard. We surfed with a piece of wood board, about four feet by three feet, like a boogie board today. It floated, but barely. You had to scrounge for your wood. Long time ago every plantation had a stable for their mules. They used to have long water troughs made out of redwood. Good boards! Redwood is almost waterproof, and it was thick. All our surfboards were different size. It depended on what wood you could find.

Tame Mischief

When I was about six or seven years old, my brothers, one older, one younger, and I were out in the sugar cane fields. I think it was a Saturday. We went up to the reservoir to catch goldfish, small little minnows. Because they were irrigating the fields that day, the water was running too fast for the fish and they were all hiding on the sides of the reservoir. So we closed the valve and then the water stayed still, so all the fish started coming out and we were catching them. Then the irrigation man came and he re-opened the valve. After he left, we shut the valve again.

Later we heard a car coming. We all hid down below in the buffalo grass. The supervisor came and he was chewing the irrigation guy out. "Who's closing the valve? How come?" The irrigator said, "I don't know but when I got here, it was closed." He opened the valve again.

The supervisor was standing on the land above us where the valve was located, looking around, but he could not see us. We were down below in the grass watching him. Then he spotted our dog running around looking for us. He said, "That's the Ibaras' dog over there. The kids must be around here."

So before we got home, the news was home already that we shut off the irrigation water. We got chewed out. Nothing bad, just enough to get our parents upset. I don't think we got really bad punishment. They couldn't stop our allowances — we never had any allowances! Think about it, that's more than 50 years ago. I know my brothers would remember that.

There were fields of coconut trees. Waimea Dairy was right there so all the coconut fields had cows in them. During the summers we used to go pick coconuts, eat them and cut down the green leaves and hide under them. The cows used to come and start eating the leaves while we were under the leaves.

I remember starting fires in the coconut fields. One man was always catching us. He always used to scold us about cutting down leaves and burning fires in the field.

I went to Waimea High School. In high school, not much to do except play sports. On Friday and Saturday nights, somebody used to pick me up and we'd go hang around at Dairy Queen in Eleele, the only thing open. We never went as far as Lihue in high school except on game nights.

When I was in high school, once in awhile they used to have roadblocks. We used to see cops standing by a light in the middle of the road and we recognized them so we'd turn our car toward them and they'd jump out of the way. They'd ask us, "You trying to get us in trouble?" That was always their question. In those days, cops were few and far between, hardly any tickets.

I guess because we were young, we never had any responsibilities, those were the good old days. You go home, food on the table, bed waiting for you. What a life, what a life. A good life.

Working for
the Plantations

Exciting Work
Bob Ritch

Bob Ritch worked for Kauai sugar plantations for almost 40 years, holding nearly every job possible at one time or another. His first job was spraying poison to kill weeds; his other jobs included "mule man," sugar processor and surveyor, as he was assigned from one plantation to another and as companies merged.

Bob still lives in Kaumakani Village in a small wooden house provided by Gay & Robinson Sugar Plantation, overlooking now-fallow fields that were once filled with sugar cane. Just beyond the fields sits the retired sugar processing mill, its hulking steel structure permanently stained red from years of iron-rich dirt blowing in Kauai's ever-present trade winds.

Bob, 60, came to Hawaii from Virginia when he was 19 years old and lived on Oahu until friends recommended he check out Kauai. Now married to his third wife whom he met in the Philippines, he helps raise their seven-year-old son. Speaking in a rapid-fire blend of his native Southern drawl and Pidgin English phrases that he picked up during his years on plantations, Bob energetically recalls his life working in Kauai's sugar industry.

You Boys Want a Job?

It was exciting work, working for the plantation. The heydays were in the late 1970s, early 1980s, everybody making money. Sugar industry was number one. We were knocking out 18 tons per acre, 20 tons, some fields 24 tons per acre. Highest yields in the world.

I started working for the plantation when I was about 22. I just moved over from Oahu. One night we were shooting basketball near Eleele, and a guy pulls up and says, "Hey, you boys want a job? Show up Monday." Sure, why not. There were four of us. I didn't ask him what the job was. When I came to Hawaii, I was like a sponge. I'll learn anything! Anything! This is living, right? I thought, "I'm out of money anyway."

They hired me as a sabidong (*Ilocano for poison*) to spray fo' kill the weeds in the cane fields. I never graduated Old Dominion University, my wrestling career was kinda pau (*finished*), so I said, "Yeah, OK, I'll learn to spray." I was a sabidong for two years for McBryde Sugar Company, and also for Grove Farm. They moved me back and forth between plantations.

McBryde had a huge 55-gallon tank that you wore on your back. The tank weighed about 50 to 70 pounds. You didn't take your tank off when you needed more poison. A driver came with a metal four-cornered bench that was high enough for you to rest your tank on and he'd fill you up, then he'd say "Go!" and you'd go, go, go. It's contract work, four acres per man. After you get through with your four acres per man on a gang of, say, five guys, it was all straight money (*overtime*).

At McBryde they paid you on the elevation of land, the steeper the more pay. They had about 13 different grades. The crew chief, the driver who filled you up, he shared the contract with you. His job was to always keep the poison going. We were going like crazy, because we tasted money.

At McBryde, if you sprayed a piece of cane, they used to charge us five bucks! I remember one guy, they took 10 bucks out of his paycheck. When he complained about it, the boss said, "You killed the cane."

The trick for spraying is you add a little soap, so it sticks to the grass, so when it rains it stays on the leaves. We used to put tons of soap. We would spray the fields in Kalaheo and kill the vegetables in Kaumakani. The drift is two miles in the air. We'd paint the fields white. Can you imagine all that flying in the air?

Grove Farm would give you a double tank, two small cylinders, and it's over each leg so your center of balance is better. You got a hose and you filled your tank yourself because your gauge was in the front not in the back. You put less air and more poison, because you got paid by the gallon at Grove Farm. And Grove Farm is flat. So we're going to make the acres and the gallons, now!

I loved Grove Farm. It was terrific. I was the only haole (*Caucasian*) guy in the fields and they were much nicer to me at Grove Farm. At another plantation, some of the supervisors, they'd talk any kine (*say anything*). It was hard knocks. It was the worst days of my life. They'd run me down. I couldn't take it. A supervisor would follow me all over the place, threaten me all the time, "If I catch you surfing, I fire you!" I wasn't surfing. I had to put food on the table.

Every Job on the Plantation

I worked just about every job on the plantation. I was the last mule man for McBryde. I had a crew of about 10 or 12 wahine (*women*) who had the mules. We only had one good mule and one semi-good — you know mules — and two or three running around in the corral, used in ancient times before. They would put pula pula (sugar cane seedlings) in baskets on the mules and we'd plant the empty spots in the fields to get a full crop. There has to be at least 90 pieces of cane in a line for every 100 feet to get good production.

I was "senior pan floor man," the sugar processor, for 12 years. You boil sugar and it crystallizes. It's like honey, you leave it on the shelf long enough and it crystallizes. On the plantations, they speed that up with steam and vacuum. You had to know exactly how long to boil the sugar and when to pour it out. It's sort of an art. One pan I had for making the sugar was from 1917 and the gauges were from then, too. But they worked! When I started that job, they gave me a crinkled up book, looked like the Declaration of Independence. You touched it and it crumbled. The formulas were written in German. I tried looking some of it up, but I couldn't read it. Some of the old timers taught me how to do it. It's like cooking: a pinch here, a pinch there.

I had a lot of other jobs. I moved equipment back and forth during a merger. I drove the mud truck at night, taking mud flushed from the evaporators out to fields that needed better dirt. I drove the two trash trucks. I was the garage clerk, ordering all the big machinery, doing all the clerking work in the garage. Then they threw me back to sabidong.

After I learned how to drive a truck, I became a haul cane truck driver. That was fun, come flying down the mountains, rockin' that load! It was 50 tons of cane, big, big. The mill was flying, grinding cane fast. They want that load down there not in 40 minutes, they want you down in 20 minutes! Twelve grabs of cane from the fields would fill the truck.

They had a habit if you're low in seniority, they'd give you a hard job. "Oh, Bob, you go over there and cut seed for a couple months." Okay, that ain't gonna break me. I'll go over there. So I was pula pula, cut seed. When you're pula pula, you don't have to work eight hours straight. You can come out at 4 in the morning when it's cool. You've got the lights on your head, the chaps. They kept me over there for three or four months until I filed a grievance with the union.

So I've cut it, planted it, harvested it, hauled it, grinded it, boiled it and ordered the parts to get it done again. The only job I never did was loading the haul cane trucks. I became the most dangerous man in the plantation because I worked all these jobs and I knew quality.

Some supervisors never got out of the truck. They would drive around the field but they couldn't see in the middle of the field because there was too much cane on the outside. Now, the old Japanese bosses, they would walk in the field. They would even come out on Saturdays and Sundays. They lived and ate and slept sugar. If it was their fields, they used to make sure every piece of cane was growing.

As plantations started to go downhill, they gave up on quality. I learned at Old Dominion University about economies of scale. Keep it small, keep it honest, keep it going. I think they could have kept operating if they hadn't gone big time.

We're Living Now

I was on the list for five years before I got this house in 1985. I said, "Now we can save money. We're living now." The place I was living before was a plywood shack I built with drip irrigation. The rent was like $15. We got over here and wow, now we got water. They took the rent out of my paycheck, $35 a month then. I pay $161 now. I have a $50,000 view of the ocean.

They built these houses in the 1960s. They decided to build the camp here because it was a marginal field. There's no topsoil, only clay. I think out of the 200 houses, 170 are pensioners. Since they closed the plantation, they kept a crew of four or five maintenance guys to do repairs on the houses. That's a wonderful thing about the

Robinsons *(owners of Gay & Robinson Sugar Plantation)*. Cradle to grave, they really take care of their people.

When I moved in, it was all Japanese in my row of houses. All the Japanese had nicknames: Birdie, Goose, Humpty, Oly because he drank Olympia Beer, Cowboy. I never knew their real names. They all passed away. My friend Smalley, because he's small, is the only one remaining.

In 1994, Bob was diagnosed with Guillain-Barre syndrome, an autoimmune disorder in which the body's immune system attacks itself, and he became paralyzed. He was in rehabilitation on Oahu for nine months, then returned to Kauai, while still remaining a member of the plantation's labor union. As he gradually regained his strength and mobility, he attended Kauai Community College for three years, earning degrees in electronics, facilities engineering and hotel management. Bob then returned to Gay & Robinson Sugar Plantation, taking a job as a surveyor.

They told me, "You know Bob, there's only a couple jobs you can do over here, if you come back. One of them is the surveyor job and you're gonna have to take it or aloha." The union told me, "You better take the job or you've got less than a month to get out of the house."

The plantation couldn't find anybody in two years for the surveyor job. They had posted the job, but you gotta read maps, and everybody was afraid. They couldn't read a map. I had two sets of maps, the ancient maps which Mr. Robinson gave me; they were from the 1920s. They showed all kinds of stuff. Then I had a newer set of maps.

The guy before me had a truck, but they told me, "You're walking." I carried the transit and I got a belt to put the flags inside and any kind of little instruments I needed and strapped it on like Batman and away I went.

Surveyors make the contour lines for the planter. You go into the fields after they've ripped it and it's harrowed then it's prepped and ready fo' go, then I come in and survey and shoot the flags. The section head tells me where the weak spots are, where he didn't get good production. He wants more contour in those sections because it was either too steep or not steep enough. I started making it so the planters could plant from this corner all the way to the other side by keeping the lines going straight.

Supervisors kept telling me, "Gotta get it into the ground fast. Bob, we've gotta get that crop in the ground before Thanksgiving. Let's go!" In the last few years of the plantation, they wanted to lay everybody off during the off-season. Labor was a big expense.

It Was Good Fun

I was an outdoor guy, growing up hiking the Appalachian Trail, living in the mountains, going on my mother's farm. But I wasn't learning nothin'. Then I come here, it was like another playground. I'm learning, people teaching me stuff. The mind keeps learning more, more and more stuff.

Working for the plantations, it was good fun.

Now I Do What I Want

Hatsuyo Sasaki

Hatsuyo Sasaki sits in a chair outside the front door of her daughter's home in Kalaheo, and beams a sweet smile that lights up the neighborhood. At 94, her youthful, almost unlined, slightly tanned face belies her age as does her full head of white hair, combed back stylishly. Her handshake is strong and firm. For 20 years she worked for Gay & Robinson, Inc. sugar plantation, beginning in the late 1950s.

Hatsuyo speaks in the present tense of Pidgin English, making her point with as few words as possible, as she recalls her time working in the sugar fields.

I start work in fields when sixth grade. I like go school but my father say, "No." I have to help family. I fight with my father. Sometimes I run away to school. But my father tell me go back work.

I carry bags of seed and carry seedlings to replant. Carry seed bags over shoulder, like this (*motions over her shoulder*). Had to cut seedlings just right and then you pile it up, pile it up, then tie it up. That wasn't very easy, you know. But we did it anyway.

In cane field I did lot of different kine jobs. No matter how hard I worked, I never did perspire.

My hands come like this (*demonstrates a claw-shape*), all those years holding knife. I no can put my fingers straight. One day this woman say, "Try massage your hands." I try. I massage every day.

Hatsuyo Sasaki full of vitality at 94 years old.
(Photo by Pamela Varma Brown)

Now I can make straight like this (*shows her straight fingers*).

Even though I come old, my body tired, this is the happiest time of my life, because no one tell me what to do. Most of my life, I have to do what someone else want. Now I do what I want, and I like.

We Take Care of You
Holbrook 'Hobey' Goodale

*Holbrook "Hobey" Goodale, the great-grandson of William Hyde
Rice who owned Kipu Plantation, lived at Kipu for 15 years, from 1941
to 1962, minus several years attending school on the U.S. mainland
and serving in the U.S. Army. The property was primarily a ranch but
eventually 1,200 acres were put into sugar production. Hobey recalls
his time working at Kipu Ranch and Plantation.*

My great-grandfather bought the property when Princess Ruth
Keelikolani called him in 1872 and asked him to buy Kipu Kai Ranch,
3,000 acres including Haupu Mountain for $3,000. What a bargain!
It's probably worth $30 million now.

My father died when I was 4 years old. I worked for my grandfather on the ranch. That was a challenge, especially without a generation between us to serve as a buffer. I was dealing with a hard head.
Oh, both of us had hard heads. Eventually I changed my approach
and created situations so he would think he came up with an idea,
then he'd turn around and recommend it to me.

I did everything on the ranch from shoveling manure and clear-
ing ditches to working in the sugar fields. At that time the plantation
had about 60 employees. They cut sugar cane by hand using a machete and loaded the cane on carts to go to the mill.

I worked for five months in the sugar fields. I was the foreman.

Hobey Goodale, circa 1947.
(Photo courtesy Hobey Goodale)

The workers were Filipino. Most of them spoke pretty good English. I only had trouble with one guy. They told me to be careful because sometimes he gets upset and would say, "I'm going home," and then the whole gang would go home. He tried that on me because he broke one of the rules. Everybody just laughed at him as he went home. A little less than a week later he was back, very hangdog. They didn't give him the time of day after that.

We harvested our last sugar cane in 1942. The head luna (*supervisor*) was dying so my grandfather sent me out. I didn't have any experience. My grandfather hollered things about my intelligence and told me I wouldn't know what to do because I was so young. The cut cane luna said "Hey Mistah Hobey, no worry. We take care of you."

A Good Life

Wilfred Ibara

Wilfred Ibara is the third generation in his family to work for Kauai's sugar plantations. He worked for Kekaha Sugar for almost 20 years as a design engineer, and for Gay & Robinson for seven years leading tours of the sugar fields and mill. Now 70 years old, soft spoken with a sweet disposition and a clear perspective of sugar's role on the island, Wilfred reflects on his plantation years and the sense of community that existed when sugar was king on Kauai.

My maternal grandfather was brought in from Japan as a plantation laborer and he started working in Kaumakani for Kauai Sugar Company before it was Olokele Sugar, long before Gay & Robinson bought Olokele. After my grandfather finished his contract at Kaumakani, he moved the family to Hanalei and he started farming rice.

My mother was born in one of the camps that is still being used today, across from Makaweli post office and mauka (*toward the mountains*), named Camp 6. When she was growing up in Hanalei, she had to work in the rice fields.

My father was born in Waimea and he worked at Waimea Sugar Mill Company for almost 50 years. He started as a mechanic. He worked his way up and became the automotive mechanic shop superintendant.

Living Like Kings

I was brought up in a Waimea Mill Camp plantation house, provided by the plantation. The housing was good. Supervisory housing was on the highway. I actually grew up in the back housing until I was 3 or 4 years old and then we moved to the front highway house. My mother said they stayed there for close to 50 years, until the plantation went out of business, which I think was in the 1960s.

This is a story my mother told me: One day the plantation office manager came by to talk story (*chat*). He told my mother, "Rose, this house has only two bedrooms. With six kids, two bedrooms for your family isn't big enough." So he was the one who helped us move to our nice big plantation house with four bedrooms. At the time of growing up, it felt big, but you walk in there today and everything's so small and cramped. But in those days it was nice. Three older boys in one bedroom; two girls in one bedroom; parents in one bedroom. My mother had an extra room for her sewing room. We were living like kings.

The company maintained the housing so any kind of work that was needed, just call the plantation up and they sent someone over. We had a lot of trouble with our cesspool. It used to back up. But all my mother did was call the carpentry shop and they'd send somebody over. They'd stick a small piece of dynamite in the cesspool and it would go boom! I guess that breaks up all the sediment, and water would come out.

After the plantation went out of business, my father was too young to retire. I think he got some politician's help to take classes at Kauai Community College to learn blueprint reading and he took carpentry lessons. He ended up as a carpenter for contractors on Kauai. My mother worked at Waimea Post Office as a clerk. After that they bought a property up Waimea Valley, built a house, and that's where they ended up. They had a good life.

After high school, Wilfred lived on the mainland, where he attended the University of Idaho for four years, served in the U.S. Army for two years, worked in the aerospace industry in California, attended courses at University of California at Los Angeles (UCLA), got married and had two daughters. He knew when it was time to return home to Kauai.

One day one of my girls came home from school in California and she said, "Somebody took my lunch money." I said, "I think the girls would be better off if we moved back to Kauai and they went to school there." I know they could have survived but I always wanted to come back to Kauai, and that was my excuse.

I came back without a job, started looking around, and ended up working for Kekaha Sugar Company on Kauai's west side as a design engineer. I was doing drafting and designing buildings and equipment. We made most of our equipment except the huge vessels and really sophisticated equipment like turbines and steam generators. We processed sugar for about eight months and the remaining time of the year, usually winter months, we did repairs and maintenance, took the whole factory apart, then we started again.

I stayed there almost 20 years until the plantation was getting shaky. Amfac (*then owner of Kekaha Sugar*) was trying to figure out how we could survive. They knew we couldn't, so they brought in tons of consultants and got rid of the managers. So I said, "Time to leave."

Before the plantation went out of business, they started selling off their real estate. I bought one of the managers' houses and I took time off for about two years, mostly playing golf.

After going back to work at a bus service, then as a foreman at Kiahuna Plantation, Wilfred found a job that perfectly combined his knowledge of the sugar industry with his affable personality.

Gay & Robinson Sugar Plantation was looking for a plantation tour guide. I said, "It's close to my retirement, I'll go take that job." I *was* retired while doing that job! We did two tours a day and in between we had a tour into some of the Robinsons' private land up in Waimea Canyon. Really nice.

It helped me understand the tourist business more deeply. A lot of customers said they learned something. A lot of them kept in touch with me after they went back to the mainland, and that was cool. A lot of people came back, did the tour again, and brought friends. They left me a lot of tips. In fact they left me so much tips, I never had to use my salary. I saved a lot of money while doing the tour. I worked there for about seven years.

At one time, there were close to 50 plantations in the Hawaiian islands, though some of them were small. Gay & Robinson was the highest yielding plantation in the world because of the weather and the water. It was the last plantation on Kauai. People would ask, "Is it going to last?" I would say, "I don't believe it's going to last very long." The plantation stopped its sugar cane operations in 2009.

Volleyball & Beer

My favorite plantation memories are of the social life. Waimea Plantation, where my father worked, was small. We used to have two parties a year. Pau Harvest (*finished with harvest*) was a hoolaulea (*celebration*) where they would roast a pig. Every Christmas they had something at the manager's house: food, presents. Big deal for those times, yeah?

When I worked at Kekaha Sugar, I was part of the supervisors' club. It was nice and close. We did a lot of things together. Every Wednesday night, we supervisors used to get together at the manager's house to drink beer and play volleyball. They started having tournaments with different plantations, supervisors' club against supervisors' club. It got big and it involved the other islands as well. Every year there was a tournament on a different island.

Every Wednesday night we practiced. Sometimes it used to last up to about 10 or 11 o'clock at night on a work night. The superintendents used to show up for morning meetings, go home, take a nap. Supervisors had to stay and work with a hangover. There are some stories about those days.

One time after volleyball we were drinking beer and somebody said, "Let's go to Oar Oar," a bar in Waimea that was where the credit union is now. So everybody jumped in a car. This one guy from the mainland was our electrical supervisor. He said, "I need a ride." I said, "You can go with me."

Waimea Dairy was still in operation in those days and they still had cows in the pens. As we passed the dairy, he said to me, "I can wrestle those cows." He'd had a few to drink. I said, "You can?" He said, "Yeah!" I turned the car around and went over to the dairy and said, "OK, go at it." He climbed the fence and he fell down in the mud and whatever the cows had left in the mud. Then he grabbed a cow around the neck. But these are all tame cows, yeah? The cow just stood there and looked at him. And he fell again.

I said, "Come on let's go. You're not a cowboy. You cannot wrestle a cow." He climbed back out of the cow pens. Then we went to the bar. Some of the guys were already there. And there he is, mud and cow's doo-doo all over him. We sat down and they said, "What happened to him?" I said, "He wanted to wrestle the cows so I took him to wrestle the cows." We had a few to drink then everyone left. I didn't see who took him home.

The next day, I found out that when he got home, he was all covered in mud, his pants were ripped from climbing over the fence. His wife called around to find out what happened to him. Through the rumors going around all day, we figured out that he walked all the way from Waimea to Kekaha to get home. He didn't remember what happened. I don't understand how people can get that wasted that they don't remember anything. But in those days, hardly any cops. Otherwise if we had gotten pulled over, we'd be in big trouble.

One day I'll tell you some more plantation stories, but those are all X-rated.

A Good Life

I think the plantations did a good job of taking care of their people. That's why the people stuck around. They gave medical care. I believe what kept me at the plantation was the housing. The pay wasn't as good as the outside, but with the housing, that was a big, big plus.

The Robinsons (*owners of Gay & Robinson Sugar Plantation*) are letting people stay in their plantation housing. In Kaumakani Village, there are a lot of retired people living there. That's a good thing about the Robinsons. They're very loyal to their workers and former workers.

Most everybody worked hard on the plantation. There were some ugly jobs. But the plantation had a different mentality, too. There were separate groups: supervisors, management and the bargaining unit, because the union split them apart. The union was almost like the enemy of management. They were always bucking management to get benefits for the workers. Workers always thought the plantation owed them something, but the plantation tried to take care of the people.

If the plantations were still here, if the salary was competitive with outside, I would recommend it to young people. The plantation was a good life.

Chicken Nuggets

Frisky Fowl

The moment Kauai people were asked if they had any stories about their encounters with the island's wild roosters and hens, tales came pouring in. Residents have a love-hate relationship with the plucky poultry, some adoring the frisky fowl while others wish the males of the species could learn to tell time instead of crowing all hours of the night and day. There are so many roosters and hens roaming Kauai that visitors from urban areas of Oahu have been overheard remarking, "Kauai, so country!" Kauai's fowl population is far larger than on the other Hawaiian islands because the mongoose, a natural predator, does not live here.

Chickens originally arrived in Hawaii more than 1,000 years ago, introduced by Polynesian explorers who brought them in their sailing canoes as a food source. In the 1800s, with the influx of immigrant laborers who came to work for Kauai's sugar plantations, chickens continued to be integral to the island lifestyle as food and also for gambling, as some people trained roosters to fight each other. (*Cock-fighting has long since been outlawed in Hawaii.*) Hurricanes in 1982 and 1992 further spread the chicken population, tossing flimsy rooster shelters and distributing the birds hither and yon.

Kauai people know the difference between roosters and hens, but for convenience, refer to all of them as "chickens," relying on context of conversations to determine if the fine feathered friend under discussion is male or female. Here are some nuggets of what it's like living on an island where chickens are part of the fabric of daily life, followed by three stories of chicken aloha.

KFC the chick cuddling with Nalu the bunny.
(Photo courtesy Becky Hallman)

KFC

Our son, John, raised all kinds of animals while growing up on Kauai. On many occasions unbeknownst to me, he would catch little chicks at Lydgate Park and sneak them home in our car. One of his favorites was a rooster he named KFC. When KFC was just a chick, John would put him in our rabbit Nalu's cage where KFC loved cuddling up to his surrogate mom. Even as a fully-grown rooster who crowed obnoxiously in the wee hours, KFC always gravitated back to Nalu's cage as his home.

— Becky Hallman

Cocksure

I have loved observing the chickens in my 30 years on Kauai. One day I bought my eight-year-old grandson, Tony, a double-scoop ice cream cone while we were strolling on a wooden plank walkway fronting stores in Koloa on the South Shore. When he said he did not like the coconut flavor of his top scoop, I told him to drop the ice cream onto the street where a cat I had spotted under the walkway would lick it up. The cat took one lick. Just then, a mother hen and several of her chicks leaped on that ice cream, chasing off the cat and demolishing that scoop in seconds.

Another time I was walking through a field to the big surfer's beach, "Pakalas" on the west side. I stopped short when I saw an enormous bull staring at me. He had big horns and there was no fence to separate us. I decided to mind my own business and walk forward. The bull made no move, he just watched me. However, in my distraction I failed to notice that I had come between a hen and her chicks. She gave me Hell. I was in more danger from the chicken than from the bull!

— Genora Woodruff

Vocal Offenders

It's always funny when I'm on a business phone call with some-one on the mainland from my office that is in a small building next to my home, and they'll blurt out, "Um, was that a rooster I just heard?" Like most Kauai residents, I no longer hear them most of the time, so I'll think back for a moment, and then acknowledge that they did indeed hear a rooster, just outside my office, during working hours.

The next thing I'm usually asked while on the phone is, "How many chickens are in your backyard right now?" Once I looked out and responded that there were "Ten or twelve at the moment." This leads to a brief history of how hurricanes Iwa and then Iniki redistributed the chicken population around Kauai, and how some resorts hire businesses to collect and remove wild chickens from their grounds, only to release them in the interior of the island. I believe this is a formal chicken relocation program that includes new identities for the most vocal offenders.

— Ed Altman

Mother Hen

I have done a lot of gardening and yard work in my 36 years on the Garden Island. In doing so I have come across many families of chickens: the rooster, hen and anywhere from one to 10 chicks. My sudden presence startles them. The rooster, he is the first one out of there, making a beeline for the nearest bush or neighbor's yard. He's the real chicken of the family.

The mother hen is totally the opposite. She will stand up to me and protect her little ones like any mom would. She puffs up and spreads her wings to make herself look larger and does a circle dance — I have not figured out the reason for that maneuver, maybe to make me dizzy — all the while calling out commands to her little ones to head for cover. If I come a little too close, the mother moves toward me and I sometimes imagine her flying at my face. If that happened, I would become the chicken, hurrying off to join the rooster in his hiding place.

— Dr. Robert Zelkovsky

Mable

I once had a pet chicken named Mable who kept me company when I worked from an office in my home. Mable would sometimes hunker down on my shoulder and preen my hair while I was on the phone. One day I was wearing only my bathrobe, negotiating challenging contract terms with the president of a large hotel company over the telephone, when Mable took a big poop down my back.

I immediately stripped off my robe but stayed at my desk buck naked until I finished my phone call. When I finally got off the phone, I started laughing and couldn't stop.

About a year later, I bumped into the man I had been speaking with on the phone that day. He asked me, "Are you OK now? Last time I talked with you, you sounded a little stressed." He lived in Hawaii so I told him the story and we shared a big laugh.

— Cathy Zadel

Golfing with Chickens

When I hear Kauai's living alarm clocks go off at 4 or 5 in the morning, I know it's time to head for the golf course. Some golf courses are chicken-friendly and the chickens know it because they follow you to every hole. One day, as I teed off on Hole 6, a rooster decided to cross the tee box. The rest was history. All I saw was feathers flying and the rooster limping off into the bushes. I felt so bad. Then someone yelled, "Hey man! You got birdie!"

— Elizabeth Suenaga

Rambo

When I first moved to Kauai more than 20 years ago, my then-husband, Herman, our neighbors and I thought if we could trap and remove an extremely loud rooster we had nicknamed Rambo, we would have quiet nights.

One morning, our neighbor, Hans, proudly announced he had caught and disposed of Rambo. But at 2 o'clock the next morning,  Rambo's unmistakable crows let us know he was still alive and well. A few mornings later, our neighbor Mike told us he was sure he had gotten Rambo with a shot in the night, and that he had seen Rambo lying in the yard. Rambo was nowhere to be seen that day. But sure enough, at 2 a.m., Rambo again announced his full life.

Finally Herman went out in the dark one night and took his shot, absolutely positive he had dispatched Rambo for good. Unable to find the body, we waited for the ear-splitting nightly crowing. When it came, we all agreed that Rambo had earned his name for his ability to survive, and his right to continue to rule our neighborhood continued for many years.

— Dale Rosenfeld

Mango Drunk

Back when I lived in a shack under a mango tree in Moloaa, there were many free-range chickens running around. When I'd come home, they would normally scatter as I approached them in my car.

One time, I pulled into the driveway late at night and saw many chickens in the headlights, sitting on the ground, not moving, but not dead and not getting out of the way like they usually do. They were just kind of paralyzed, seemingly stunned by the headlight glare. I had to get out of the car and actually move them out of the way. In doing so I noticed many over-ripe, half-rotten, half-eaten mangoes also on the ground. Evidently those chickens had become quite intoxicated from eating the rotten mangoes.

At daybreak the chickens were gone, but it was a strangely quiet morning.

— Eric Torgerson

Love in the Walmart Parking Lot

It all happened in less than 40 seconds. Traffic in the Walmart parking lot halted from three directions. Drivers seemed paralyzed, not knowing whether to remain stopped, honk their horns or go forward in the hopes the lovers would move. Customers entering and leaving the front door stopped in their tracks, some giggling and covering their mouths. There was a brief public sense that this moment of fowl intimacy should not be interrupted.

A young boy innocently asked his dad, "Is that a cock fight?"

"You might say that," came the father's mumbled reply.

Delivering a strong elbow jab to her husband's ribs, the boy's mother said, "Only on Kauai."

And then, as fast as it began, it was over.

— Dr. John Wichert

Kauai Chicken Soup Recipe

Set a pot of cool Kauai spring water on the stove.

Add:
4 carrots, peeled and sliced
1 onion, peeled and sliced
4 stalks of celery, roughly chopped
1 bay leaf
1 Hawaiian chili pepper
1 Kauai chicken
1 three-inch Kauai lava rock, rinsed

Bring all ingredients to a boil. Reduce heat and simmer gently for 5 hours, until you have a rich, fragrant broth. To serve, throw out the chicken and eat the rock.

— Marta Lane

Crowing Companion

One day a neighbor's dog got ahold of a rooster and was rolling it in the road. I chased the dog away, but by the time I arrived, the chicken had already lost all its feathers. I brought him home and put him in a box. I thought he was going to die.

The next morning the chicken wasn't moving too well, but he was crowing. I fed him and in a couple of days he started walking again. After awhile I let him loose in the yard, where he would walk around and make himself comfortable, eventually becoming strong enough to jump in our big mango tree.

That chicken and I became good friends. I found him three days after my girlfriend, Diane, had left on a business trip. When she returned home, I said, "Look at my new friend." He came right over and crowed for her. Diane said, "Oh, cute little chicken." I know he liked her. Whenever Diane woke up in the night, the chicken would crow for her. Every night it crowed and crowed.

You couldn't help but admire him. For being a chicken, he had a great attitude, wasn't aggressive, was very gentle, and always came when I called. It sounds crazy, but I really liked that chicken.

One morning, he didn't come when I called for him in the yard and we haven't seen him since. We hope he found a good new home. We will always remember him, though it's a lot quieter around here now.

— Keala Kai

Dusty

By Mika Ashley-Hollinger

Mika Ashley-Hollinger has lived on Kauai since 1983, is co-owner with her husband, Stuart, of Kupono Landscapes, and is the author of "Precious Bones," a book published by Random House about a young girl growing up near the Florida swamps. She shares a story about chicken aloha.

My husband and I have the pleasure and privilege of living in a pristine valley on the North Shore of Kauai that is alive with an assortment of endangered ducks, birds and feral chickens. From our vantage point we are able to observe all the natural interactions between these feathered creatures. At times, it's like living in a National Geographic moment. I like to call it Chicken World.

Believe it or not, we have seen just about every human emotion expressed by chickens: love, hate, jealousy, fear and grief. We can go out in our yard and call a chicken's name and it will come running to us just like any other pet animal. Chickens do not have night vision. That's why you never see them after dark unless they are sick or injured, but they do have a keen sense of hearing. They can detect and remember the slightest sound, whether the scraping of a can that means food, or the click of the hammer on a pellet gun that means harm.

Over the years we have rescued countless chicks and injured birds who remember us for the rest of their lives. One such chick is Dusty, who was a pathetic little black fuzz ball about two days old that we found lying in the grass in a shopping center parking lot, so sick it could not stand or lift its head. We brought the chick home and nursed it back to health. In a week or so it was running around our house peeping and playing, following our every move like a little puppy. But Dusty was stunted and didn't grow, just a tiny little creature with a couple of black feathers sticking out here and there, the rest of its body still covered in black fuzz. We couldn't tell if it was a hen or rooster. Dusty was truly an ugly chickling!

When Dusty was one month old, we brought home three one-day-old Sebright Bantam chickens. We placed them in our makeshift incubator, which is actually a heated aquarium, the same place where Dusty had spent the first couple weeks of life. Dusty was fascinated with the babies, sitting on the outside of the aquarium, making little mother hen peeps with such a look of longing that I finally placed Dusty inside with the babies. They immediately bonded. They ate, slept and played together and became an inseparable family. Dusty seemed like a proud, protective mom.

With all this chicken love, Dusty flourished, and over the next month began to grow and develop feathers. Then it became obvious that Dusty was a rooster! He eventually grew into a stunningly handsome black and white fellow. He roosted in the coop with the bantams until he became too large to fit inside. He still stays with them all day and makes sure they get in their coop at night. If we bring home any rescue babies, Dusty runs up the stairs and sits for hours with them. He loves the hens and has quite an entourage, but his true calling is that of a loving, caring single dad!

Chickens sometimes get a bad reputation because they are so misunderstood, but they are actually intelligent, social beings that create strong family bonds. They are very entertaining and make great pets.

Mr. Rooster

By Cynthia Justus

Cynthia and Ed Justus own Talk Story Bookstore in Hanapepe where they have several cats and share the neighborhood chickens.

When my husband, Ed, and I lived on the east side of Kauai, we lived near a pond where we had a few ducks that we raised as outside pets. They loved the pond and would also come to eat out of our hands near the duck food bin we had nestled between the groves of banana trees. Eventually, the ducks must have spread the word about these cool digs and free food because other ducks came waddling down the street to join the club.

Shortly thereafter, a beautiful black and red rooster with a full comb, large wattles and a gorgeous tall tail came to participate in the feast, but he attacked the ducks to have all the food for himself. Ed chased him away, telling him, "You can't come back until you're nice!"

A week later, the rooster returned, sauntered into the yard, but instead of attacking the ducks when the feeding began, he ate along with them politely. We welcomed him to stay and we named him "Mr. Rooster."

A few months later, after Mr. Rooster had become a regular in our front yard menagerie, I looked outside and saw him lying on the ground on his side. I thought he was dead! When I ran out to check on him, he quickly got to his feet and looked at me as if to say, "What's going on?" We had never seen a rooster so relaxed that he would lie down and take a nap. Clearly he was very comfortable with us.

It was right then and there that I fell in love with Mr. Rooster. I think it was mutual. He would knock on our screen door looking for me. I would say to him, "Hello, my big handsome rooster!" and he would reply with flirtatious clucking and strut proudly back and forth across the front porch.

One day, some months later, we hadn't seen Mr. Rooster all day. Suddenly I heard the blood-curdling scream of a chicken and I just knew it was him. I ran out of the house in the direction of the scream and found myself at the neighbor's fence across the street. To my horror, the neighbor's huge pet German shepherd held a screaming Mr. Rooster in its jaws. I begged and pleaded with the neighbor to please let me get our rooster. The neighbor just told me to go away, that his dog had caught Mr. Rooster and that was it. I shook the neighbor's gate until it broke open and ran in. Again, I pleaded with the neighbor to spare our rooster, explaining that he was our pet and very special to us.

Eventually the neighbor got his dog to release Mr. Rooster from its jaws. Mr. Rooster fled the moment he was free, but in his blind haste, he trapped himself between a bush and the fence. I scooped him up in my arms, and for the first time ever I held a rooster. He remained calm as I carried him back over to our yard.

Though he was in some degree of shock, fortunately all that Mr. Rooster had lost was his "pride," his beautiful tail feathers, leaving just a bald stump. Once home, I said to him very clearly, "You stay over here from now on. If you go back over there, I may not be able to save you next time." He obviously understood, because from that day forward, he never wandered from our yard again.

Shortly after the incident, Mr. Rooster amazed us yet again. As his "pride" started growing back in on his rump, about twice a day he would walk around the outside of our house until he found which room I was in, sit below that room's window and serenade me with a lovely continuous song. I never knew roosters could make such gentle sounds. It was a soft warbling croon with a melody all its own that went on for about 20 minutes. His show of affection touched me deeply and endeared him to me even more.

Eventually, we moved to another home but Mr. Rooster remained on the property with the ducks. We still think of him fondly and he will always hold a special place in our hearts.

As the Egg Turns

Lori Kunkel

Lori Kunkel lives in Kapaa on the east side of Kauai, where she once owned pet hens but is now thrilled to enjoy quiet anonymity among feral chickens.

As my mother and I sat on the lanai of my home in the heart of old Kapaa town, a feral chicken with seven little chicks came up to us. Most feral chickens don't get too close to people, but my mom liked feeding them and they started hanging out at our house. Oh, boy.

I live on a very busy street with a lot of traffic. One by one, six of the baby chicks ran into the street and got run over. That left the last chick alone with no brothers or sisters. We named her Chick Chick. When her mother abandoned her, as hens do once their offspring reach a certain age, Chick Chick became very lonely.

Mama Chick went across the street, had 10 more chicks, then came back, strutting through my yard, wanting me to take care of her and her new babies. She always hissed at Chick Chick, who wanted so much to be part of a family that she basically stalked her mama.

One day, Mama Chick was crossing the road with her 10 young-est, with Chick Chick following close behind, when boom! A big jacked-up truck with huge tires came zooming by and hit Chick Chick. Feathers flying everywhere! It was awful. I was very upset.

Amazingly, Chick Chick was alive but she was freaked out. She hid under some bushes. Her tail feathers were completely knocked out and she had one severely broken leg that was just dangling. Peering under the bushes, I said to her, "I'm so sorry that happened to you and I hope you make it." The next day I couldn't find her. I just assumed she went somewhere to die.

The following day, there she was right outside my door. In her weakened state, the other chickens in the yard began picking on her, so I relocated everybody else to protect her. I took Mama Chick and her 10 babies to a field down the way where they could have a good life.

Chick Chick continued to live in my yard and I fed her very well. Her feathers slowly grew in. Her leg got better, little by little. It took months. For a long time, when she flew up into the night-blooming jasmine tree in the evenings where I could check on her, she would cry because her leg still hurt.

Over time, she healed amazingly well. Her healing was so magical that I decided to change her name. I called her Chi Hen. Chi means energy. She even began laying eggs. I told her, "You're like a phoenix who has risen out of the ashes."

Right around this time, I adopted two domestic chickens, Goldie and Rosebud, and life around here began to resemble a soap opera. I called it, "As the Egg Turns."

I gave Goldie and Rosebud a little outdoor house I called the Hen Hilton that didn't have a floor and that I could move around so they could peck at the dirt and fertilize different parts of the yard. Chi Hen really wanted to be friends with them, but Goldie would only be kind when Rosebud was laying an egg. One day somebody stole Rosebud, and Chi Hen and Goldie became buddies. Chi Hen, originally feral, found her way into the Hen Hilton and began laying her eggs in the nest box that was meant for the domestic chickens.

She wanted to be part of a family so badly that she sat on her eggs all the time, but without a rooster to fertilize the eggs before she laid them, no chicks were going to hatch.

Funny story about the Hen Hilton: I normally moved it several feet every few days but one summer day, a friend suggested we move it under the cherry tree so it would be in the shade. The chickens were out hunting at the time. When they returned, they couldn't find the Hilton. It was only 15 feet away. Finally they went to the last place it had been and the two of them sat right there, next to each other, as if it was still there. I never moved the Hilton that far in one day again.

About this time I realized that chickens were a little too much work for me. They were coming to me all hours of the day yelling for food. I couldn't even lie down and take a nap. I decided to give them away to friends who have a pond.

I brought Goldie over first. I was worried that the other chickens on the property might be territorial and unfriendly, but the moment she entered the cage where Rudy the Rhode Island rooster was, he mounted her. Goldie became Rudy's main hen and she was instantly accepted into his flock.

Shortly thereafter I brought over Chi Hen. She became best buddies with Henrietta the Hen's chicks and was very happy to have brothers and sisters.

I visit Chi Hen now and again. She will come right up to me and sometimes she will sit on my lap. She doesn't limp anymore. You would never guess she had such a horrible accident when she was younger. And now she has a family of her own: three baby chicks. She loves to show them off to her family of two-legged friends and let us hold them.

My life has returned to being quiet and low-maintenance. I am so happy that Chi Hen now has chicken friends, family and roosters. She's a little bit spoiled, but if any feral chicken deserves it, she does.

Kauai &
World War II

The Day the Army Arrived on Kauai

By Ray H. Smith

Ray Smith was a nine-year-old boy living in Koloa when soldiers from the U.S. Army arrived on Kauai on a quiet weekend morning, four months after Japan bombed Pearl Harbor on Oahu, pulling Hawaii into World War II.

We're in Hawaiiya, Ain't We?

I remember the exciting moment when U.S. Army trucks first rolled into Koloa on April 1, 1942 as if it were yesterday. My father was the pastor at Koloa Union Church; he and my mother had been missionaries in China. We had come to Kauai six months earlier, after a year on Oahu.

Our church's parish hall was commandeered to serve as the mess hall for successive Army units that were shuttled in and out of Koloa until late 1944, for their jungle and assault training.

Rows of wooden barracks had been hammered together to house several hundred former National Guardsmen from New York on the grounds of Dr. A. H. Waterhouse's estate, today the site of Koloa Missionary Church and a residential subdivision. Two big latrines had been dug and washhouses built immediately on the other side of the four-foot high stone wall which separated our parsonage from the new Army camp. I never heard my mother complain about her new view, only 35 yards from her front door.

As the soldiers piled down that day from the trucks in their uniforms and large backpacks, sweating and parched in the humidity, they spotted a group of wide-eyed, barefooted Koloa School fourth-graders. In their thick New York accents they said, "Hey, yourse, can you get us some pineapple juice? We're in Hawaiiya, ain't we?"

Pulling out coins and bills from their pockets, groups of military men crowded around us and began placing orders. For the next two hours, we ran a shuttle service back and forth to Usa Store for cans of juice and bottles of soda pop until the store ran out. I netted over $10 from miscounted change and tips, equivalent to 10 months of allowance at my going rate of 25 cents a week!

The Strangest Pidgin You Ever Heard

Many years later, as a retired journalist living in Wheaton, Illinois, I was lying in bed one night reading "And Blow Not The Trumpet," a 304-page book by Stanley D. Porteus published in 1947. It was primarily about how the Territory of Hawaii's civilians coped during wartime, and included an entire chapter devoted to Kauai.

While reading Chapter 12, called "Pakiki Na Kanaka Kauai," translated as "Tough are the men of Kauai," I let out a yell, startling my wife: "I'm in here!"

Here is what the book passage says:

> To GIs from New York State, this island in the Pacific was as foreign as the Philippines or New Guinea. The people seemed to be of all breeds and colors but equally unin-

telligible. Even the whites didn't know north from south, but uttered some strange gibberish about "mauka" (*inland*) and "makai" (*toward the ocean*). No wonder that when one group came into Honolulu and saw an armed Japanese guard watching the Hawaiian Electric power house, one of them yelled: "Hell, boys, let's go home. They've taken the place."

Of course the unintelligibility was not all on one side. One white child, the son of a former missionary to China, was completely mystified. "Father," he said, "those men from Brooklyn speak the strangest Pidgin you ever heard."

Do I remember saying that? No. So how could an unknown grammar school boy in short pants surface in a serious history on World War II?

Most likely my father used my declaration as a humorous sermon illustration from his pulpit, and Dr. Porteus, a professor at the University of Hawaii, heard it repeated by the many soldiers training in Koloa who attended our church services.

I probably uttered a version of that sentence when I came home with my fistful of money, jubilantly unaware of the real significance of the arrival of armed forces on Kauai and of how the 31,000 men, women and children on Kauai rallied to support their country in its time of crisis.

Unwavering Loyalty
Kauai's World War II Veterans

When Japan bombed Pearl Harbor on December 7, 1941, plunging Hawaii into World War II, thousands of Hawaii-born Japanese American men joined the U.S. Army to defend their home against the country of their parents' birth. But the War Department, fearing disloyalty, soon re-classified those soldiers as 4C, "Enemy Aliens," stripped them of their arms and told them to return home.

When the War Department later decided more soldiers were needed, Hawaii's Nisei *(first generation of Japanese born in America)* responded by the thousands and the all-Nisei 442nd Regimental Combat Team was formed. The 442nd was soon combined with members of the 100th Infantry Battalion, comprised of former members of the Hawaii National Guard. Together they became known as the 100th/442nd.

The 15,000 soldiers of the 100th/442nd were sent to some of the bloodiest battles of the war. They fought valiantly, and with their "Go For Broke" motto, became the most highly decorated units in U.S. military history. Together, the Japanese American men of the 100th/442nd earned more than 18,000 individual decorations for bravery including 9,500 Purple Hearts, awarded for injuries incurred during wartime, 560 Silver Stars, 4,000 Bronze Stars, 52 Distinguished Service Crosses, 21 Medals of Honor and 8 Presidential Distinguished Unit Citations.

Japanese Americans also supported the United States in the Military Intelligence Service (MIS), translating captured Japanese documents for the U.S. government, a service that is widely credited for shortening the war by two years, saving billions of dollars and at least one million American lives.

Sixty-six years after World War II ended, members of the 100th, 442nd, and the Military Intelligence Service were honored in a Congressional Medal of Honor ceremony in Washington, D.C. in November 2011, finally officially recognized as the Americans they had always been.

Among the World War II veterans who made the long trip from Kauai to Washington, D.C. to receive their Medals of Honor are Turk Tokita, 91, Kazuma Monty Nishiie, 96, Norman Hashisaka, 86, and Jiro Yukimura, 90.

What follows are these four men's stories told with their own brands of humility, passion and a touch of humor. Their courage and bravery represent all of Kauai's veterans.

Honored as Patriots
Turk Tetsuo Tokita

Turk Tetsuo Tokita smiles as he holds up a newspaper article show-
ing a photo of himself wearing a white ginger lei and saluting after re-
ceiving his Congressional Medal of Honor during a ceremony held in
Washington, D.C. in November 2011. The newspaper headline reads:
"'Enemy aliens' now honored as patriots." Without a trace of bitterness
at the almost seven decades it took for him and his colleagues to be for-
mally recognized by the government that they had served loyally, he says,
"This is what I looked forward to, that we would be honored as patriots."

Turk, 91, was born and raised in Lihue, not far from where he now
lives with his wife, Emi. The ninth of 11 children, he grew up in Kaipu
Camp in a small house built for sugar plantation workers by Grove
Farm in the early 1900s. As slim as when he was a soldier, with a sweet
smile and sweeter disposition, Turk reflects on enlisting in the 442nd,
fighting overseas, and why it was important for him to help Hawaii
become a state.

My grandfather was with a Samurai castle in Japan. In those days,
they used to fight a lot. His castle lost a battle so they were all supposed
to commit suicide. Instead he gathered his family and took off to Tokyo, jumped ship and came to Hawaii. He became a paniolo *(cowboy)*
at Parker Ranch on the Big Island of Hawaii, then he came to Kauai
where he worked for Grove Farm. He died when I was eight years old.

When I was in my early 20s, I worked part-time at Lihue Japanese Christian Church with Rev. Paul Ozumi. While I was working there in 1941, the Japanese bombed Pearl Harbor. The military police took Rev. Ozumi from his home without even telling him why, just took him to prison. I asked permission to visit him to discuss church matters, but the military people wouldn't allow anyone of Japanese ancestry to see him. I thought it was terrible discrimination.

When I was 21, I volunteered to be drafted into the U.S. Army. I

thought it would do some good for my family and friends and for the community. I was stationed at Schofield Barracks on Oahu and worked as a supply clerk. After about six months of work, I was given a seven-day pass for time off. I flew home to Kauai.

On my fifth day on Kauai, I had a funny feeling. I thought, "I better go back." So I called, and they said "We'll put you on a plane if you come in tomorrow morning." Early in the morning on my sixth day of leave, wearing my U.S. Army uniform, I went to the office in Eleele where they gave seat assignments for flights out of Mana, on Kauai's west side.

I waited all day. They wouldn't put me on the plane. They told me, "We don't have any room. Come back tomorrow morning." There were all these Caucasians. Why were they letting all of them get on?

I went to the office the next morning. I waited and waited and they wouldn't put me on. I said "You've got to put me on or I will be Absent Without Official Leave (AWOL) if I don't report back by Monday morning." They looked me right in the face and said, "We don't have room for you."

I called my captain and told him, "I can't get on the flight. Can you do something for me?" He said, "No, I can't do anything for you. You get here by tomorrow morning 6 o'clock or you're going to be AWOL."

On Monday morning I went to the office in Eleele again. Finally at 10 a.m. they let me get on the plane. By the time I reported to Schofield Barracks, it was already around 12 o'clock. The captain told me, "You're restricted to barracks. We're going to charge you with being Absent Without Official Leave and you're going to be court-martialed."

Just before I went out of his office, I looked up and saw this big sign on the wall asking for cadres (personnel) for a newly-forming unit of the 442nd combat team made up of all Japanese ancestry. I looked at the captain and said, "What if I volunteer for that outfit?" He said, "If you're out of here today, pack yourself and move, we'll drop all charges."

You know what I did? I rushed back to the barracks, packed my things and boom! I was out of there. That's how I got into the 442nd. I'm happy that happened because I got into the 442nd. That was in 1943.

Fearing treason, the U.S. government had imprisoned more than 120,000 people of Japanese ancestry across the country; many had been U.S. citizens who had owned homes and businesses.

The mainland boys who joined the 442nd, they had a hard time because their families were in the internment camps. The Hawaii boys were very free with their money, treating anybody to drinks. But the mainland boys, they didn't want to drink or buy candy or nothing.

I asked some of them, "Do you not have money? Are you getting paid?" They said, "Money? We send every penny we have back to our parents."

When we were in Mississippi for training, we used to go into the forests and countryside. We would see these poor white people out there and they weren't treated too well. Why all the difference? How come? There were also Blacks-only bathrooms, Blacks wouldn't be allowed in certain restaurants and they had to sit in the back of the bus. It was shocking to see.

They were supposed to be Americans, and they were being treated like they were slaves or something. They didn't have the same opportunities.

Turk earned the first of his two Purple Hearts in 1944 outside the small village of Bruyeres, France, population approximately 3,000, that had been under German control for four years. The 100th/442nd set the town free, but half of their men lost their lives in the process.

Bruyeres was all hills and mountains and thick pine trees. We went up and down fighting the enemy. The Germans knew exactly where we were because they were there first and then withdrew. They used to throw a lot of artillery and hit the pine trees. The trees would burst and shatter all the shrapnel. Anybody within 50 or 100 feet would get injured.

We were attacking a hill. The Germans attacked us with a lot of artillery and that's when about 15 of us got injured. I was wounded in the back and it hit my shoulder blade. One piece of shrapnel about four inches long traveled about six inches toward my spine and stopped about one inch before my spine. Fortunately it didn't come through to my chest or I would be dead.

Turk and other soldiers wanted to go to Biffontaine, the second small French village the 100th/442nd had liberated that month, to seek emergency treatment, but Turk had earlier heard German machine gunfire along their normal path. He advised the others that it would be safer to take a different route, but men who were carrying stretchers said it would be too steep. A soldier from Sacramento, Calif., joined Turk on the alternate route. Together they slid about 500 yards down the mountain where they reached a field of waist-high wheat.

We started to walk about 50 yards or so when we heard machine guns. We ducked and crawled. I said to the guy with me, "See that? That's exactly where they're going with the stretchers." We crawled about 200 yards. They fired at us. We had to walk about a mile and a half back to Bruyeres. He and I were the only ones who made it back.

When we got to the first aid station, they said, "The others are coming. We're going to wait for them." I said, "No sense in waiting. They've been captured." They said, "They're coming back." I said, "They're not coming back." Then they shot us so full of morphine, we passed out.

The next day I woke up in a field hospital with about 150 of our boys in various stages of dying. I was there quite awhile, waiting.

It was maybe the next day when they finally took me in. They shot me full of morphine again. I was on the operating table and they said, "We ran out of anesthetic. Is it all right to operate on you?" I said, "Go ahead." They put something in my mouth to bite on. All I remember is the first cut.

Next time I woke up, I don't know what day it was, but there was a pastor or minister, waking me up. He said, "How you doing son? Here's a Purple Heart for you because you were wounded." I said, "Thank you." He said, "And here's the shrapnel that we dug out of you."

I said. "Thank you," and blam! I threw it. I was so mad. Then I passed out and next thing I knew I was in a hospital in the south of France.

I don't know how many blood transfusions I got. A month and a half later, I came down with hepatitis, yellow jaundice. I was really sick. They thought I was going to die. I asked the doctor how could I have yellow jaundice. "Must have been tainted blood," he told me. I couldn't eat much. Oh, I was really weak. I lost so much weight.

I wish they had sent me home. But they wouldn't allow us to have anybody else but Japanese Americans for replacements. And we just didn't have enough boys.

After the battles of Bruyeres and Biffontaine, the Japanese American unit was ordered to save the "Lost Battalion," a group of 211 Texas soldiers of the 36th Division who had been stranded for days on a ridge in France, surrounded by German soldiers. The 100th/442nd successfully broke through the German line but in five days of fighting, lost 800 more men in the rescue. After all three battles in these small French villages, the combined unit had lost more than two-thirds of its men to wounds, capture and death, and many more were never found.

Three weeks after Turk's injury, the wound in his back still bleeding from residue shrapnel that doctors had been unable to remove, he was sent back to the front lines, supplied only with bandages and instructions to change them daily and to keep the wound clean.

The 100th/442nd was ordered to Italy. Turk earned his second Purple Heart in a battle around a German-occupied castle. When the Germans fired a cannon, Turk jumped into a deep hole the Germans had dug earlier for themselves.

I heard the cannon. I looked back. All our boys were in the road. I yelled, "Get in the hole! Get in the hole!" While I was doing that — Boom!

A shell came, knocked out my teeth and put me out of action again.

During training, our members of the 442nd always said, "Let's go for broke. Let's throw everything in, nevermind we die or not." We knew we weren't going to come back.

When Turk returned to Kauai after World War II, he was lost.

You get used to a certain type of life. It was hard to get assimilated into regular civilization. I used to drink a lot to forget what happened.

I had, still have, tinnitus, ringing in my ears. As section leader, I had to crawl in front of machine guns and direct the fire, so they used to fire over my head. I was about 10 feet in front of them. You know how much noise there is from guns? I used to be deaf, really deaf after coming off the line. For the first three or four days, I had to write everything down. After awhile I could hear a little bit, but until this day I have ringing in my ears.

I was interested in photography and I went to a photography school in Los Angeles for one year. It wasn't really satisfying. I went to the Institute of Design in Chicago. I studied painting, sculpturing, photography, cinematography. They told me that if I finished my fourth year there, I would get my degree in art.

In 1947, my back wound was still bleeding. It wouldn't heal. I went to the U.S. Department of Veterans Affairs (VA) in Chicago. The doctor looked at me and asked, "Are you an American citizen? Where you come from? Hawaii? Where is that?" I knew I wasn't going to get anything from him. He didn't know where Hawaii was. That really convinced me that Hawaii had to become a state.

I was already signed up for my fourth year at the Institute of Design. One day I was eating Italian bread in Chicago, and boom, my two front teeth cracked and fell off. I went to the Veterans Administration and told them, "This is a war wound." They said, "There's nothing on your record that says penetrating wound." What does penetrating mean? I went to a dentist who told me, "The cheapest thing I can do is $1,500." I said, "What? I can give you only $300."

I said, "I'll come home and see what I can do." I went to a dentist in Hanapepe on Kauai, who was very sympathetic. He said, "I can do it for $175." I had to borrow the money from my sister. I was that broke. He gave me a dental partial.

About 20 years later, when I had to get a bridge put in, it was going to cost $7,500 and the VA said I could only have it done in Honolulu and I would have to stay there for three or four weeks. I live on Kauai. What I'm going to do in Honolulu for three or four weeks? I wrote my congressman, Daniel Inouye, who also served in the 442nd, and who was then a senator from Hawaii. I sent him X-rays and a formal quote from my Hanapepe dentist. He got it approved to be done on Kauai. It was fortunate I knew Dan Inouye.

After Turk returned to Kauai from school in Chicago, he became involved in politics, seeking more opportunities for the people of Hawaii, then only a territory of the United States.

After my experiences with the doctor and dentist in Chicago, and from visiting New York, I was convinced that Hawaii had to become a state. I figured it was the only way we were ever going to get anything.

I went to Honolulu where I met Dan Inouye, Patsy Mink and others who were campaigning for John A. Burns to become a delegate to Congress. Burns promised us if he couldn't get statehood in two terms, he would never run for office again. He got elected for the first time in 1956. In 1959, he got us statehood. When I found out, I said, "Oh, boy. Really? My God!"

Burns became Hawaii's second governor. He was our governor for 12 years. I was his Kauai campaign manager for all of his terms. I was Kauai campaign manager for three more Hawaii governors after Burns.

Before the war, I was an introvert. If you knew me before the war, you'd think, "What a wimp he was." Because of politics, I became an extrovert. My life really changed. I helped with statehood and became involved in all kinds of things for a better life for everybody.

We Had to Prove Our Loyalty
Kazuma Monty Nishiie

Kazuma Monty Nishiie, 96, an original member of the 100th Battalion, is still trim and alert, his small frame barely a wisp over 5 feet tall, posture as straight as when he was a soldier. His alert eyes take in everything around him. He speaks seriously and thoughtfully, occasionally inserting wry humor into his responses with little change in facial expression. The secret to his health and longevity? He points skyward and says, "The man above," then pausing for effect, and with a slight hint of a mischievous grin, says, "and young wife." Celia, his "young wife" sitting next to him, laughs heartily.

Before responding to questions, Kazuma pauses, seeming to review images in his mind, recalling events that took place almost seven decades ago. He speaks in short, compact sentences, using the bare minimum of words required to get his point across.

My father was born in Japan. He came to Kauai as contract labor for Kilauea Sugar Plantation. Transportation in those days was very bad. Many months on the ocean. Took long time. Terrible conditions.

My father worked hard, long hours. My mother was picture bride. She came from Japan, met my father when she got off the ship. She was a teenager. I am oldest of 10 children, five girls, five boys. My mother, with 10 children, lot of work. Large family. Very hard living. *(Shakes his head at the memory.)*

When I was a boy, I fished at Kilauea Beach, caught papio, ulua, moi. We used tree branches or twigs for fishing poles. More fish then than nowadays. Hunted pig, too.

I went to work for the plantation when I was 15. All my small earnings went to support the family.

Kazuma was drafted into the U.S. Army in 1940. Soon after he became a member of the original 100th Battalion, a unit comprised entirely of Nisei, the first generation of American-born children of Japanese parents. One of Kazuma's younger brothers also joined the military. When Pearl Harbor was bombed by Japan, emotions ran high throughout Hawaii.

It was terrible, you know. Parents' country bombing Pearl Harbor. Because our parents were living in America, they knew the children must be American, must be faithful. They used to tell us, "Do your best in the service." We had to prove our loyalty.

Kazuma was sent to the American Midwest for training, where he found the absence of his dietary staple of rice particularly disorienting. Most Japanese people in Hawaii had eaten sticky white rice daily since they were children.

From the very beginning, went to the mainland, not enough rice. Because our top officials were local guys, white officers *(from Hawaii)*, they really hustled and got us some rice.

After basic training, they shipped us to Italy. We were part of a large convoy, oh many, many ships. Had to zig zag to keep away from the German submarines. Conditions on ship were terrible. So many people, crowded, couldn't get up. When they threw up, made you throw up, too. Very long trip.

When the 442nd Regimental Combat Team arrived in Italy, we joined them to take the place of their First Battalion that had remained in the United States. The War Department was good enough to let us keep the 100th Battalion designation, so to this day it's always 100th/442nd.

Kazuma was wounded in 1943 near Monte Cassino, Italy, where a monastery also called Monte Cassino, sat atop a hill.

I was on the mortar platoon. I helped fire an 81 mm mortar. You stand around the gun. One person drops the shell into the barrel, the shell hits the firing pin and the shell flies out. The mortar is not a direct firing weapon. It goes up and over, so the gun crew cannot see the enemy or the explosions.

When we went on the hill, we could see Monte Cassino but the Germans could see us, too. *(He pauses, focusing on disturbing images from more than 60 years ago.)* The Germans had already zeroed in on the place where the troops would pass. So right away, they threw a barrage and we had heavy casualties. It was terrible.

I was injured on my right arm and both legs and feet. They brought me to the hospital. When I became well, the management didn't send me out or discharge me. They kept me in the hospital to take care of the laundry department. Everything has its day.

Kazuma was awarded a Purple Heart for his injuries. When he was discharged from the U.S. Army in 1945, he returned to Kauai, where his job at Kilauea Sugar Company as "pan man," the man who boiled the plantation's sugar cane juice to turn it into sugar, was awaiting him. He says with a wide smile, "there's no place like home."

Everybody was happy I came home. My father was still alive and working as a rice farmer at Kilauea Stream.

Many veterans returned with what they call "shell shock." I spent my time outside fishing and hunting, let the mind forget the war. I think it helped me.

In 1953 I got married first time to Keiko. My parents and her parents came from the same place in Japan. She was born in Waimea, Kauai, brought up by her auntie and uncle in Japan because they had no children. We got married in Waimea. Simple, simple, simple wedding.

Secret to long marriage? Don't argue too much.

Keiko passed away in 1992. Approximately six years later, Kazuma was given the name of a schoolteacher in the Philippines named Celia. For almost five years, they corresponded by writing letters and by telephone. After they met in person in 2003, Celia returned to the Philippines to complete her 26th year of teaching. She returned to Kauai later that year, and she and Kazuma were married. She is the "young wife" whom he credits for his health and well-being.

They playfully joke about which one of them caught the other. "She catch me," he says. "No," she says laughing, "the Kauai boy caught the Filipina city girl."

Celia: When I came over here, we got married, May 28, 2003. In one of his letters he said he is a "veteran" but I don't know what kind because he did not tell his age before. He wrote, "I am ____ ?"

Kazuma: I have a problem: very talkative wife *(laughs)*.

Upon learning of his military service, Celia has ensured that her husband has taken part in veterans events, where he is warmly welcomed and clearly well-respected by all other veterans in attendance, men often reverently pointing him out to others. In 2011 he took part in the 79th National Convention of the Military Order of the Purple Heart in Minnesota where he was recognized by General Eric Shinseki

Kazuma and Celia Nishiie dancing at the Old Soldiers of Hawaii Reunion on Kauai in 2011.
(Photo courtesy Bob Goodwin)

*Kazuma Monty Nishiie, at age 96, giving credit to the man above
and his young wife for his health and longevity.
(Photo courtesy Bob Goodwin)*

(Ret.), *then U.S. Secretary of Veterans Affairs who was born and raised
on Kauai; the 22nd gathering of the Old Soldiers of Hawaii Reunion;
and the Congressional Medal of Honor Ceremony in Washington, D.C.*

Kazuma *(With a broad smile, then looking down shyly):* I'm very
proud and very happy.

We Thought of Ourselves
As Americans

Jiro Yukimura

Jiro Yukimura, 90, is a happy man, speaking animatedly with a broad smile and easy laugh, his arms sometimes sweeping the air, his small wiry frame full of energy. He grew up in Lihue in the 1920s and 1930s, on the southeast shore of Kauai, where he still lives with his wife, Jennie.

Pearl Harbor was bombed while Jiro was in college. He quickly joined the U.S. Army, only to be rebuffed shortly thereafter due solely to his Japanese ancestry. He eventually found a way to serve his country, joining the Military Intelligence Service.

Oh, childhood on Kauai was carefree. We could go wherever we wanted to go. There was no such thing as "no trespass" signs. We could roam all over the place.

The only place we had activities was at our church. You know what our Christmas present was? Two apples, one orange and some hard candy. We had no presents like the way the kids have these days.

We spoke English and wrote English at school. There was also a Japanese school that we all went to for an hour every day after school, so we had some knowledge of the language, and of course our parents spoke Japanese. But, you know, as kids, we went to the Japanese language school more for fun than to learn.

In those days the so-called haoles, or white people, were plantation managers or department heads, all big shots. My dad was a cook
for Sheriff Rice. There were a lot of advantages for us growing up in
that kind of setting. The sheriff had a beach house at Haena on the
North Shore so every summer he would load us in the car and drive
all the way, starting out in the morning. The road was terrible com-
pared to what it is now. By the time we'd get there, I'd be sleeping in
the car. Every summer we spent three months going to the beach and
just fooling around. It was a great time. I got my love for the North
Shore from those days.

*Jiro was attending the University of Hawaii, Oahu, living with oth-
er students from the neighbor islands, when Pearl Harbor was bombed
on December 7, 1941. He and some of his friends decided that because
they had two years of ROTC training and knew how to handle a gun —
a 1903 Springfield rifle, .30 caliber, to be exact — they would volunteer
for the U.S. Army.*

My first assignment was to go to Ala Wai Yacht Harbor near
Waikiki on Oahu to watch whether the Japanese would start to at-
tack us. That night they gave us a gun, all right, and they gave us only
one clip and one clip holds five rounds. So what you going to do? If
the enemy should come, you going to shoot the five rounds and then
you take off? We guarded the yacht harbor, a water tank in Wilhelmi-
na Rise and an electrical station.

After about two months we all got assembled at a school, and
they said, "All you Japanese guys, you're out." They said they cannot
trust those of us of Japanese ancestry. We all cried. They classified us
as 4C: Enemy Alien. We were considered enemy alien? My God, that
was a big blow. So we all went home. What else could we do?

One year later, the U.S. Army desired more manpower and called for Japanese Americans to serve. The government hoped for 1,500 men from Hawaii and 1,500 from the mainland but was flooded with 10,000 Japanese American volunteers from Hawaii, then only a territory of the United States.

We were so anxious to get in. We thought of ourselves as Americans. We were all wanting to participate. We wanted to be treated like anybody else.

We were worried about our folks, but they were more worried about us. They said, "If you gotta go, you go and fight for your country."

After the basic training was just about over, the interviewer came from the Military Intelligence Service and wanted to see how proficient we were in the Japanese language and he brought us a third grade reader. About 250 of us pulled out from the 442nd and went to Camp Savage up in Minnesota where they had a Japanese language school.

After six months of intensive Japanese language studies, we got shipped overseas but they didn't tell us where we were going. We headed toward Hawaii so we sang Hawaiian songs . . . and then we passed Hawaii *(laughs)*, and ended up in Sydney, Australia.

From Sydney, Jiro was sent to the Allied Translator Interpreter Service, which was just beginning in Brisbane, Australia. For eight hours each day, he translated Japanese documents that U.S. soldiers brought back from the front lines or retrieved from Japanese soldiers who either had become prisoners or who had died.

Eventually there were about 2,000 translators in Brisbane. It was just like going to class. You start at 8 o'clock, take a break, get through at 5 o'clock and go home.

We all did individual experience with different units, Army, Navy, Air Force, Marines, whomever you were assigned to. We were all scattered so that every unit that fought against the Japanese had some interpreters with them. After you finish your job, invading some island or so on, then you come back to rest and start all over again.

After six months in Australia, Jiro was shipped to New Guinea, and also served in the Philippines, where he got to have a little fun.

As a matter of fact, I got to know a couple of pretty Filipino girls there and they tried to teach me some Filipino songs. (*He breaks into a Filipino song about love.*)

On August 6 and 9, 1945 the United States dropped atomic bombs on Hiroshima and Nagasaki, Japan. On August 15, Japan surrendered, ending World War II. Jiro was fortunate enough to attend the surrender ceremony held aboard the battleship USS Missouri on Sept. 2, 1945.

Just about that time they made me an officer and just about the same time they attached me to the public relations office. The PRO handled all the correspondence, all the media people. Lucky for me. So when we moved into Japan, I went with the correspondents.

We got on our destroyer and went up to the middle of Tokyo Bay where the Missouri was. We found we were assigned to a deck. Ringside seats. I didn't have any official duty. I was just like a tourist sitting there and watching the scene. I felt like the war was officially ending right there before my eyes, and I was thinking, "Now we can go home."

Americanism Is
A Matter of Heart
Norman Hashisaka

Norman Hashisaka, 86, grew up in the small coastal town of Nawiliwili, Kauai, a stone's throw southeast of Lihue. Tall, slim, soft-spoken and scholarly, Norman reflects on his experiences in World War II, serving the United States in the Military Intelligence Service as a Japanese language translator both during the war and after the war's end during war crimes trials in Yokohama, Japan. Norman now lives in Kalaheo with his wife, Mabel.

My father arrived from Japan in Hawaii around 1904 to work on a sugar plantation, first on Maui, then Oahu, then Kauai. He eventually started his own business. He was quite an entrepreneur and wanted to get into truck farming and raising vegetables and things like that.

We didn't have a lot of toys like children have today. We had to make our own things. We used to make rafts out of banana tree logs and play like Huck Finn and Tom Sawyer. Or we'd go down to the beach and go surfing. There were no surfboards like there are today so we had to use plain pieces of wood to body surf.

I wanted to go to college badly but had to raise some money. To pay tuition was such a problem in those days. I heard the Military Intelligence Service recruiters were in town looking for people with some knowledge of Japanese. I did go to Japanese school for one hour a day after school. I wasn't that fluent but I grew up in a Japanese-speaking family so I could communicate. But I knew very little written Japanese. I knew how to write simple kind of Japanese: girl, a person, a tree. The recruiter examined my test results, and surprisingly, he said I passed.

One of the things that attracted me was the GI bill. After you serve for 2 or 2½ years, the government will pay your college tuition and some living expenses. I said, "Wow, that's what I'm interested in. I'd be glad to go into the service and willing to serve in whatever capacity and I'd sure like to go to college whenever I come back." I got inducted January 3, 1944.

Uncle Sam would take us inductees from Hawaii to Camp Savage, Minnesota for Japanese language training. We landed in the middle of January. We'd never seen snow in our lives. I remember one morning snow piled up against the barracks door and we couldn't open the door. That was a shock. That was quite an experience, but we survived.

The training was very intensive. Day and night you read, write and speak Japanese. We learned how to interview prisoners, intercept messages, monitor radio broadcasts and analyze captured documents.

After training, Norman was assigned to the Philippines, where he and his U.S. Army colleagues unintentionally traumatized Filipino citizens, who panicked seeing Japanese faces arrive on their shores.

When the Japanese had occupied the Philippines, they committed all kinds of atrocities and mistreated the people. Seeing us brought back horrible memories to the Filipinos. When we arrived in the Philippines, we were greeted with horror by the citizens, who pointed at us and cried out, "Japon! Japon!" They were shocked and terrified to see us because even though we had the American uniform and carried the rifle, we looked Japanese. We were told not to go out into the towns by ourselves, to always take a haole (*Caucasian*) soldier with us, sort of like a bodyguard.

You see, the MIS soldiers like us serving in the Pacific, we faced triple jeopardy. Were we to go up to the front, we could be captured and tortured or shot by the enemy. We could also be shot by our comrades by mistaken identity. And if it was jungle warfare, we could be shot and killed by the natives. This was the situation for Nisei soldiers.

One day while I was in the Philippines, a call came to the company platoon I was in that a 10-man team of translators was needed to go to Okinawa. We all volunteered. They picked the 10 men. I wasn't one of them. They left early morning on the day before the war ended. The tragic news came back to us that the plane crashed in Okinawa. From what I read about the conditions that caused it, the airfield was so full of smoke from all the Allied bombings that the pilot couldn't see. On his third attempt to land, the plane crashed into the bluff or part of the mountain. We lost all 10 of our MIS interpreters including one boy from Lihue, Kauai. His name was Kazuyoshi Inouye. That was really sad.

After the war ended, you're thinking, "Wow, we're happy the war ended, but we lost so many."

After the war, Norman was sent to Japan as part of the occupation troops. He was eventually assigned to translate during the war crimes trials in Yokohama in which prisoner of war camp commanders were prosecuted for torture of American, British and Australian prisoners. Most of them were sentenced to life in prison; some were hanged.

The crimes were atrocious. It was a very unpleasant kind of work. The most difficult part of that job was the families of these people who were on trial. During the break they would approach us and ask for help because we were of Japanese ancestry so they could communicate with us. All we could do was say, "We'll do the best we can to interpret and translate whatever the proceedings are."

I did that for about five or six months. As soon as my time was up to be discharged, I was offered civilian jobs to remain in Japan. But I said, "No, thank you. I'm going home."

Actually, I wanted to attend college. That was one of my motivations to volunteer initially for the military, because of the GI Bill benefits. Without that, many of us couldn't go to college, couldn't afford to. I attended University of Hawaii at Manoa on Oahu. I majored in psychology. It helped me understand individual behavior.

For almost 30 years, the work of the Military Intelligence Service was classified by the U.S. government. During that time, Norman and the 6,000 other Japanese Americans who served in the MIS were unable to talk openly about their wartime contributions.

In November 2011, a Congressional Medal of Honor ceremony was held in Washington, D.C., recognizing the service performed for the United States by members of the 100th Infantry Battalion, the 442nd Regimental Combat Team and the Military Intelligence Service. Although the recognition was more than six decades in coming, Norman, who flew from Kauai to the nation's capital for the event, is grateful that MIS work is now out in the open.

It's wonderful, a great feeling to be finally recognized by Congress after many years of being told that these things are classified. We're very glad we were part of the group and did whatever we could to help win the war. We tried the best we could, we worked hard, but there were others who did so much more.

The thing I feel bad about is those who never came back to receive this recognition. That's the sad thing about a war.

I think this quote from a publication by the MIS Historical Committee in Honolulu titled, "The Nisei Intelligence War Against Japan," sums up our participation in World War II: "The MIS story is about people of diverse ethnic backgrounds who served together to achieve a common goal. They validated the truism, 'Americanism is not and never was a matter of race or ancestry. Americanism is a matter of mind and heart.' "

I thought that was the last war to end all wars. But somehow we human beings have never learned. I hope some day we'll all live in peace.

Kauai's Ocean

Nothing Can Keep You From Going Out

Sharron Weber

Two-time world surfing champion and five-time Hawaii state champion Sharron Weber says that riding inside the barrel of a perfectly formed wave, also known as the tube, is the most wonderful feeling in the world. A Kauai resident for almost 40 years and owner of a rubber tire dealership for that same length of time, Sharron shares her story of being a top surfer in the 1960s and 1970s, and how her passion for surfing opened the door for her to live on Kauai.

When you're in the tube, some people call it the green room, it's the ultimate. You have the sun. You have the ocean. You have freedom. You're only in there for seconds and once you're in it, you have to have perfect trimming of your board on the wave to get through the tube. There isn't anything better in the whole wide world.

The largest wave I ever rode was about 15 feet during a surf competition at Haleiwa on Oahu in the mid-1970s. I wasn't known as a big wave rider, but you can't fear anything if you surf.

I learned how to surf when I grew up in Waikiki on Oahu. I taught myself, then I started competing. I won the junior title two months before I was 16.

I surfed on the amateur circuit for about 10 years. I went all over the world. I surfed in Australia. I won the world title there in 1970. I competed in California and won the world title there in 1972. I also surfed in Puerto Rico and Europe including France. I even had a French boyfriend.

When I was living on Oahu, I worked at a retail tire store and I was also competing in surf competitions. One day I got a call from a friend asking me to teach a little boy how to surf while his family was on vacation in Waikiki. I taught him. The next time the family was in Hawaii, they asked me to teach a younger son. And on their next time in Waikiki, they asked me to teach their youngest son to surf. I loaded up the truck with tires and did my deliveries around the island. Each day I took a different one of the three boys with me. Wherever I delivered, we would surf.

When I defended my world title in Huntington Beach, California, all three boys, their parents, my family and three or four thousand people were watching. It was nerve-racking, but I just went out and focused. My waves were small but I did the best maneuvers of the whole event. I won the world title again.

In 1974, the father of those three boys offered me the chance to run my own tire company. He asked me to choose where I wanted my store to be: Hilo, Kona or Kauai. I picked Kauai because of Hanalei and "Pakalas," my favorite surf spots. We opened Tire Warehouse on September 4, 1974, one day after my birthday.

I had to put in more time at Tire Warehouse to keep the business open, so I had less time to surf. There was a surf competition at Haleiwa on Oahu's north shore. I waited five days for the surf to come up high enough so we could hold the event, but it never came.

I had to choose to surf or to run Tire Warehouse. I withdrew from the competitive circuit. When I wasted my five days at Haleiwa, I didn't have five days to waste. You sit there waiting for the surf to happen. I didn't have sponsors in those days. Nobody did.

I don't have any regrets. Life's too short. I teach surfing some-times. Poipu is the easiest and safest place to learn on Kauai. I'm more into golfing these days. Surf spots have gotten more and more crowded with stand-up paddlers and lots of surfers. I like it nice and free, so I go more for the golf course now.

But there will always be something about surfing. On a perfect day, people will let go of everything. On a perfect day, nothing can keep you from going out.

Sharron Weber bedecked in flower lei at the 35th anniversary celebration for her rubber tire dealership, Tire Warehouse, in 2010.
(Photo by Pamela Varma Brown)

The Only Footsteps in the Sand
Kelvin Ho

Kelvin Ho is an ocean enthusiast who has sailed around the Hawaiian islands, in the South Pacific and across the equator. He enjoys conventional surfing, and his most recent passion, surf-skiing, in which he paddles downwind on waves in a one-man canoe. Kelvin, a kahu (minister), speaks about the ocean from both material and metaphysical perspectives.

What I love about the ocean is that it brings you to your limits. For some people, just putting their feet in the water or putting their heads under water is a huge, huge step. The world's best watermen have seen their limits, too.

When you are on the surface of the ocean, you have the sky above you and the ocean beneath you. We, in these body forms, are right where these two powerful energies meet and dance, and we get to hang out in that amazing in-between zone.

Sensory wise, being on the ocean forces you into the present. You're not thinking about the bills you've got to pay or what you're going to eat. You are focused because you're in the moment. It's something to aspire to, to be in that state without help, but it's nice to have the help!

I surf in just a few places. I've cultivated relationships with the living presences in these surf spots. The Kanaka Maoli *(Native Ha-*

waiian) point of view is that everything has consciousness. When I feel a presence in a waterfall or in a surf spot, that's a gift. That happens when the mind slows enough to feel everything around us.

The ocean is a source of the Divine because it's something people can never fully master. At some point you surrender. In that surrender, you unify with it and become part of something that's greater.

I think the ocean is so healing because while we're in the water, we release gravity. I believe that our souls and spirits know what it feels like to be free. Being in these bodies on land, it's weighty. When you go into the water, all of a sudden you're freed from gravity, then our souls remember who we are.

One of the things I love about Kauai is that after more than 30 years here, I know I can go to a beach tomorrow and be the only footsteps on the sand.

In Perfect Unison
By Jean Rhude

A popular sport on Kauai is competitive outrigger canoe racing, a strenuous activity in which teams of people paddle canoes up and down the Wailua River, in the ocean along the coast of the island and sometimes from one island to another.

Jean Rhude took up paddling when she was 60 years old and found a new joy in her life.

When I was 60 years old, I was invited to join one of Kauai's low-key recreational canoe-paddling clubs. I started showing up three days a week at the Wailua River. I was a novice, and fortunately our coach, Puanani Carvalho, was also a teacher who taught special needs children. I am sure this provided her with the patience to teach me.

Pua was a gifted teacher in that she made going back and forth on the same river seem like an adventure. She also organized amazing "full moon" runs, in which we paddled on the river at night under a full moon. I loved the camaraderie of being in the canoe, of finding the cadence, of stretching the limits of my body and overcoming fear.

Before I learned to paddle correctly I felt like my arms were going to fall off! I eventually got stronger but I had no desire to compete. I was very afraid the first few times we left the river and ventured out into the ocean.

Eventually our canoe club decided to enter a few boats in some of Kauai's competitive events. We practiced starting, turning and making up time after switching which side of the canoe we were each paddling on, but I didn't participate in the races.

One Saturday I got a call that our club was one woman short for an event and asking if I could come join them. I did and we won! I was hooked. I competed in every regatta that season and for several years afterward. This often meant participating in five races in one day.

When we would compete at Hanalei Bay, the beauty was over-whelming. The ocean was so clear you could see 30 feet down; the waterfalls in the mountains; rainbows arcing over the whole scene. It was breathtaking! I'd be in the middle of a heat and remark how beautiful everything was. I think they made the bumper sticker "Shut up and Paddle" because of me.

By the time I was 63 years old, I had two seasons of open-ocean distance racing under my belt. Eventually that got too competitive for me and when my grandson, Sequoya, was born, my Saturdays were transitioned to child care. Now I meet with other ladies on Sunday mornings and paddle the "Church of the Wailua."

In Perfect Unison

Here is a story I wrote describing a wonderful morning of paddling on the Wailua River with my canoe club sisters:

A downpour of tropical rain pelts my roof as I grab my paddle and toss it into the back of my car. I hope there are least six of us who will brave the rain so we can fill an outrigger canoe. It is often much drier four miles down the road to the canoe hale (*structure*). I am chilly in shorts and a T-shirt but looking forward to being on the

Wailua River again on Kauai's lush east shore.

When I arrive, the river is full, the ground wet and mine is the only car. I think to myself, "What wimps they are to let a little rain keep them away." As I run across the grass and duck under the tarp roof of the hale to escape the downpour, another car pulls up, then another, until there are five of us. I should have known my paddling sisters would brave the weather. We take the boat out one person short of a full crew.

Frances grabs the ama *(flotation "arm" of the canoe)* while the rest of us push the 400-pound outrigger canoe down the bank into the river. Pua agrees to steer. She places Rocky as stroker, Frances in seat two and me in three, Mo in four, five empty and herself in six.

We wade into the cool water and hoist ourselves into our seat. Pua yells, "Paddles up!" and we ready our blades, alternately bent forward and fully extended, waiting for the next command. "Hit!" she yells, and our paddles slice the water in perfect unison.

We each watch the person in front of us to make sure our paddles hit the water precisely at the same moment. We check our hand grip at the top of the paddles to make sure we are all in time with number one, finding the cadence that will take us to the glide that is inherent in a perfectly synchronized canoe. "Hut!" I yell. They answer with a "Ho!" that allows for a big exhale and one more stroke before the paddle is quickly changed from one hand to the other as we pour on the power for two strokes to make up for the half second we lost changing hands.

As we pass the marina and a few stand-up paddle boarders, the river opens before us and I am happy not to be racing, instead enjoying a relaxing run. I will return sweaty with my heart pounding but without the pressure of training. I will have also just burned 680 calories.

I know every curve of this river that is so sacred to the Hawaiians. Houses on the northern bank, past the bridge, the lookout where visitors watch as we traverse our way inland to the wilds where the hau bushes *(sea hibiscus)* drop their yellow blossoms onto the surface and immediately turn orange and float, creating a magical environment where we paddle through flowers and jumping tilapia. We paddle past the Hawaiian village where Kawika blows a conch shell in greeting to us.

Finally we moor at the dock of Fern Grotto where Elvis Presley sang in the movie *Blue Hawaii*, using our paddles to pull us alongside the pier and brace ourselves so we don't huli *(turn over)*. We turn to dip our feet in the water over the gunwale of the boat and drink from our water bottles. We chat like zebra doves on a fence post, sometimes jumping in for a swim.

On our way back, the current practically takes us on its own and as we round a bend, the wind nearly sends us back to the grotto. "Hit! Hit! Hit! Plant those blades!" yells Frances as she struggles to keep the canoe out of the bushes. Just as quickly, the current shifts direction and we are out of the wind. The coconut tree that marks the last mile before home is to my left. The day's first riverboats taking visitors to the grotto pass us as their passengers snap pictures of us. I sometimes wonder how many photo albums I'm in all over the world.

Once back ashore, we lift the canoe out of the river onto a bed of rubber tires and tie it down. We meet on the grass in a circle like a third grade T-ball team, one paddle in the center, and recite our team chant. I am reminded of how much I love paddling a canoe.

Just a Regular Guy Who Loves to Paddle

Vic Allen

Vic Allen hasn't let his blindness keep him from enjoying the ocean. An athlete all his life, he took naturally to competitive canoe paddling after he lost his sight at the age of 38, and is now an integral member of a canoe paddling team.

Full of joy and exuberance, Vic engages in animated conversation, moving his head and eyes the way sighted people do, turning to look at you when speaking, gesturing with his arms to indicate heights or sizes of things. With his lightheartedness and his physical size of 6' 2" and 220 pounds, muscular and tanned, Vic seems like a big, happy teddy bear.

Just a Regular Guy

I've always loved the ocean. My stepfather was a Navy SEAL who taught us to swim by throwing us in the water. By the time I was eight years old I could swim around the pier, a good mile in and mile out at Huntington Beach, California. We were thrown in boats when we were small keiki (*children*), but we didn't race them. Canoeing wasn't really a sport in Southern California.

When I was 28, I got jumped by five men outside a tavern in San Diego, California and they punctured my eyes. I lost my left eye. For

10 years I could use my right eye, until a contact lens rubbed on the scar tissue and caused a tiny hole. I caught a cold on Sunday and was blind by Monday. That was in 2005. I was 38 years old.

Once I moved to Kauai, a friend talked me into joining a canoe paddling club. I've always been a competitive person and I've always liked football and baseball. I didn't really think of paddling as a sport. But now you've got surfing and competing together. Wow, that's the best of both worlds! You're lining up and there's all that testosterone on the starting line.

Being blind is actually an asset in a waa (*canoe*) because I can feel it, I can roll with it. I lock in with my knees and actually become part of the canoe. If we huli (*turn over*), I just grab the seat and go with it so the 400-pound canoe doesn't land on me. I've hulied so many times and I always stay connected. I never let go of the canoe. It's usually my job to turn the canoe back over.

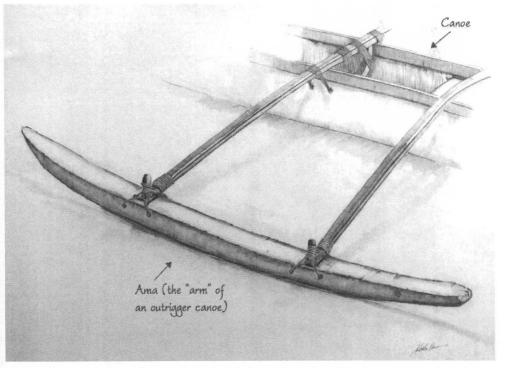

Canoe

Ama (the "arm" of an outrigger canoe)

(Drawing by Keala Kai)

I'm usually Seat 4 on a six-man team because I'm one of the bigger stronger guys. It's my job to keep the ama (*flotation "arm" extending from an outrigger canoe*) down. I'll jump out on it or I'll shift my weight to keep us from flipping over. Of course, I learned how to do all this after I lost my sight.

(*Photo by Annie McEveety-Allen*)

My first canoe race was in Poipu on the south shore. We were almost at the finish line when a rogue wave hit us and we flipped over. The crowd on the beach panicked. It was a big deal because Kauai was not used to seeing blind people paddle. I was fine. Now they know I'm just a regular guy.

Paddling is all about lokahi (*unity*), doing it together, especially on a team of six men. That's what propels the boat. One guy is not going to make that boat go; it's everyone pulling together. When everybody's on, it's smooth, just like being in a rocking chair.

I See What I Want to See

I'm a very visual person, which makes my life easier. I have two prostheses for my eyes. I don't see anything. I have no light perception at all. And yet, I see perfectly fine. I see it completely in my mind. As we talk I'm forming a vision of you.

When we're out paddling, sometimes I get in the water and swim. Of course I have to open my eyes underwater so I can see. I guess I can't really see but I do see. I see what I want to see. Pretty rocks or little turquoise fish. Sometimes I see something and say, "Look at the size of that fish." I don't know if there's a fish. Don't rain on my parade.

I attribute my resiliency and positive attitude to my mother, all 5-feet tall of her. She was a strong woman and she raised us well and to be strong. It's also my faith. I have a lot of God. I'm just a mist who's going to be a vapor soon. I know where I'm going when I'm done and it's all good.

I can't say that I've never had a bad day. I can't say that I don't get frustrated if I go in the cupboard where the peanut butter is supposed to be and nobody's there to help me and I spend half an hour looking for it only to find out it's on the next shelf where it's not supposed to be. Being blind has taught me patience and acceptance. Now I have a lot of patience.

Being blind isn't all that bad. It's like when you go scuba diving and it's a whole other world. Being blind is a whole other world and you adapt to it and you become another fish in this world.

The ocean is a huge part of my life. I've got to go in the water almost daily. I don't know what I'd do without it. I'm more comfortable in the ocean because I can't run into things. I feel calm out there. I'm just a regular guy who loves to paddle.

(Photo by Annie McEveety-Allen)

Healing Power of the Ocean

Kurt Leong, Suzie Woolway & Bruce Cosbey

One Saturday morning each month, autistic children and adults, people in wheelchairs, and stroke and other brain injury survivors, are escorted into picturesque Hanalei Bay by an army of volunteers who help them surf. As participants ride waves into shore with lifeguards, firefighters and other experienced watermen and women at their sides, their thousand-watt smiles beam their joy to be alive.

Kurt Leong's passion for surfing led him to co-found the non-profit Kauai Ocean Recreation Experience (KORE) in 2009, to help people with disabilities enjoy the ocean. Kurt grew up near the beach in Kailua, Oahu, and learned how to surf from his brothers and neighbors when he was seven years old, surfing almost every day after school. Now a Kauai firefighter, he still surfs as often as possible.

Suzie Woolway, Kurt's KORE co-founder, speech therapist, owner of Ohana Home Health and co-founder of Think BIG!, a brain injury support group on Kauai, loves helping disabled people get in the ocean.

KORE Volunteer Bruce Cosbey, a general contractor, surfer and longtime Kauai resident, has watched the ocean transform people who have disabilities.

Kurt: I wanted to start KORE because it was something I could do. I knew surfers would want to help other people experience the ocean and the good that it does a body, soul and mind. We wanted to spread that feeling to people who haven't surfed before or who used to surf and can't anymore. We have chosen a beach where small and gentle waves break over a shallow sandbar, making it ideal for what KORE does. All the participants love it. I don't know for sure, but I think our volunteers enjoy it even more!

Growing up, my brothers, my friends and I surfed because it was fun. We didn't think about it like exercise or working out. When we got to be in our 40s, we said, "Wow, we're still in good shape because of surfing." There aren't too many exercises where you can have this much fun.

It saves your soul when you surf. It gets all the negativity out of your body and mind. It's the rhythm of the ocean. I can't explain it scientifically, but it works. Being in the ocean is about being in nature, being outside, no matter what you're doing. You feel connected to the land.

Suzie: I couldn't stand that these beautiful young women and men couldn't do the things that they loved or wanted to do anymore, possibly from choices they made that changed their lives forever. KORE solved that.

KORE is for the entire family, not just the one with a disability. One of our participants is a 12-year-old who has Asperger syndrome, a form of autism. The mom also has three baby girls. Our volunteers take the 12-year-old out on a surfboard, and all three little girls want to go, so our volunteers take them, too. The mom can't do that on her own.

Really, the power of KORE is realizing how much we are all alike, regardless of how our bodies work. I look at Kauai and KORE as microcosms of how I would like to see our world evolve: realizing we're more dependent on each other, and being more accountable to each other in a caring, human way. The ocean provides us this classroom where we can all help each other and see each other as the joyful human beings we are.

Bruce motions toward an autistic 19-year-old, standing shoulder-to-shoulder with KORE volunteers who are looking at photos in a book, laughing, clearly enjoying his time with them.

Bruce: I'll never forget his first day with us at KORE about six months ago. He was extremely shy, real stand-offish. He didn't want to be touched. He needed a minimum of 10 to 15 feet space from anybody. One volunteer gently coaxed him into the ocean and on a surfboard.

He is now a changed person. Now when you see him get out of a car or off the bus in the morning, he runs to get to us. He's so fired up. He's a seal now. He can't stay out of the water.

A friend of ours who is in his mid-20s is a triple amputee. He likes to come visit our KORE ohana (*family*) and show everyone how easily he can surf, even without legs and only one arm. He often says, "Impossible is only an opinion, not a fact." That's the power of the ocean. It brings it all back.

Kauai Ocean Recreation Experience (KORE) volunteers lovingly surround a person paralyzed from the waist down so he can enjoy time in the ocean. (Photo by Pamela Varma Brown)

One Person Always Makes A Difference
John Tyler Cragg & Dr. Monty Downs

John Tyler Cragg, a soft-spoken man who owns lifeguard, swimming and CPR training businesses on Kauai and the mainland, uses Rescue Tubes in his professional capacity. When he learned that people on Kauai were grabbing whatever they could find on a moment's notice to save someone from drowning, especially at the island's many un-lifeguarded beaches, he wanted to provide something made for the purpose. Rescue Tubes were just the ticket.

Ingeniously simple, Rescue Tubes are 50-inch-long, 6-inch-wide, 4-inch-thick pieces of foam that can support as many as three adults in the water. Now installed on beaches throughout the island, Rescue Tubes seem part of Kauai's landscape, but it was John's quiet determination that started the process, and Emergency Room physician Monty Downs, who took it to the next level to make that become reality.

Monty, a surfer and doctor with an abundance of energy, first worked with John, then later agreed to take the reins. He has helped "Rescue Tubes" become a household word. John's initiative and Monty's tireless efforts have set the stage for at least one dozen lives to be saved on Kauai each year by people using Rescue Tubes.

Beyond My Dreams
John Tyler Cragg

When I started doing this in 2008, I envisioned the number of drownings each year on Kauai would decrease. But I never imagined Rescue Tubes would save so many lives. It's beyond my dreams.

When I first started putting Rescue Tubes on beaches on Kauai, I used to hang them off trees with little makeshift signs. You have to start somewhere. I had a lot of naysayers. People said they would get stolen or that there would be liability issues. I politely said, "Back off." Don't stop someone from doing some good.

Two weeks after I put a Rescue Tube at Lumahai Beach, a 15-year-old kid saved a South Carolina man who was in his 40s from drowning. The man was able to float out in the ocean with the Rescue Tube while gently kicking toward shore. It took lifeguards 20 minutes to arrive on jet skis from Hanalei Bay, the nearest lifeguarded beach at that time.

A Rescue Tube keeps a barrier between the rescuer and rescuee which is very important because you want them to grab something — that is not you — to keep themselves afloat. If those tubes weren't there, I don't think so many people would have the courage to swim out and rescue people.

There's a passage in the Talmud that goes something like: "If you save one person, you save a nation." The one person who is saved by a Rescue Tube, his progeny have children upon children and children, and some generations later, you've saved 200 people. So many people are thankful for that one Rescue Tube.

I encourage people to follow something that is in your heart that you know is helpful. Other people get behind it after they see it's working. We all have our own skills that can make the world a better place.

I Feel Tremendous Joy
Dr. Monty Downs

As an emergency room doctor, I've seen my share of dead bodies; I say a little prayer, but over my career it has become a situation that I can handle. But seeing the family of someone lost to drowning, it's heart breaking, agonizing, no matter the age. So many people are affected by a drowning. We all hurt when it happens.

On Kauai, we have some of the most beautiful beaches in the world and most of them are un-lifeguarded. We tell people to go only to the beaches that are guarded but that's not realistic for visitors or for residents.

So when I saw the Rescue Tube that John Tyler Cragg had hung at Larsen's Beach after it helped save three members of one family, a light bulb turned on in my mind that this might be something that could help.

John and I joined forces. We spent a couple of days driving around, finding suitable trees and bushes at beaches to hang more Rescue Tubes, but the vandalism rate was high and they didn't really look too sharp.

We graduated to PVC pipe, put in a few nuts and bolts to hold the Rescue Tube and a placard of instructions. Thanks to people with engineering minds, we refined the materials and the process to make installation easier and more durable.

The first few I installed took an hour and a half just to dig the holes and put in the rocks to secure the poles. Now we can do a Rescue Tube installation in about 15 minutes. We purposefully make the Rescue Tubes very easy to remove, since things happen very quickly when there is a beach emergency.

Residents have taken emotional ownership of the Rescue Tubes.

One time I went to Ke-
oneloa Bay fronting the
Hyatt hotel in Poipu to
replace an older Rescue
Tube. I left the new one
in the truck and began
taking the old one off
the pole. There were a
couple local guys sitting
at a picnic table nearby
drinking beer. One said,
"Hey, brah, how come
you taking that?" I told
them, "I've got a new
one." They relaxed and
said, "OK, brah!"

People report if a
tube at their favorite
beach is missing so we
can replace it. Private
landowners call and ask
if they can have us place a Rescue Tube on beaches in front of their
homes. One of the great things about doing the maintenance work
on Rescue Tubes is that I get to see all the beautiful beaches on Kauai
that I might not otherwise go to that often.

Each Rescue Tube set-up costs only about $100. One tube lasts
on average two years on Kauai with our salty ocean air, so we turn
over about 90 tubes per year at a cost of $55 per tube. Our financial
vehicle, so to speak, is the Kauai Lifeguard Association, a 501(c)(3)
non-profit corporation, and also the Rescue Tube Foundation, Inc.,

that was started by members of the Rotary Club of Hanalei Bay.

Originally my vision for Rescue Tubes didn't extend beyond Kauai, but thankfully other people, including those with the Rescue Tube Foundation, had greater vision and now Rescue Tubes are being used on other Hawaiian islands and even on the mainland.

Kauai's unlifeguarded beaches are so tantalizing and so well publicized, but they can create catastrophe — very quickly — for us and for our visitors. Our hope is that Rescue Tubes will not only continue to be directly helpful in rescues, but also that their presence will have a cautionary and preventive effect.

I feel tremendous joy knowing of families that are still whole because one or more of their members were saved by someone using a Rescue Tube.

Hold on Dad, I'm Coming!
The Garvey Family

When 16-year-old Taylor Garvey visited Kauai from Southern California, with his parents, Kevin and Su, and his younger brother, Torrey, the last thing he expected was to rescue his father from drowning at one of Kauai's beaches. Fortunately, Taylor knew exactly what to do when he realized his father was in trouble. By a stroke of luck — or was it fate? — he had watched a water safety video playing in the baggage claim area of Lihue Airport.

The family's harrowing day took place at Kaakaaniu Beach, commonly known as Larsen's, a beautiful, secluded and unlifeguarded beach on Kauai's North Shore.

This is Safe

Kevin *(Taylor's father):* This was probably our seventh time visiting Kauai together as a family, and I have been coming to Kauai since the 1980s.

Larsen's Beach was not on the regular rotation of places that we like to go. I read about it in a Kauai guidebook. I saw that it was a somewhat dangerous swimming beach and to avoid the channel.

We saw the sign at the beginning of the trailhead that said, "Dangerous Swimming Conditions: 13 Drowning Deaths," but we didn't plan on doing a lot of swimming or snorkeling so we thought it would be fine. It was pretty deserted; there was only one person in the water.

I don't like to go to unknown beaches without having a sense of where things are, so I walked the length of the beach to get a sense of where I thought the channel was. Taylor followed about 100 yards behind me. When he saw there were some clothing-optional people, he turned around and went back to where my wife, Su, and younger son, Torrey, 8, were relaxing on the sand near the end of the trail.

I perceived the channel that the guide book warned about was roughly two-thirds of the way down the beach, and we were easily within the first one-third of the length of the beach, so I thought, "This is safe."

I have some beach experience having grown up in Southern California. I've bodysurfed, boogie boarded and surfed a little bit. I wasn't unaware of the danger. I had no intention of putting myself into a dumb tourist situation; it just sort of evolved.

I began by snorkeling in shallow water, near the only other swimmer. The water was only about three feet deep above the reef. It was pretty and the water was clear, yet it was really kind of claustrophobic. So I decided to swim out a little bit to see if I could find any drop-off. I have done this before at other beaches and been fine.

Just as I headed out a little farther, a rush of water swept me out beyond the reef into deeper water and to the open ocean. I was a little bit concerned being out that far, but I didn't panic, even though it was a little disconcerting. It took me a minute to kind of calm down. There were bigger fish out there, and I thought, "This is cool." A minute or two later, I realized I didn't feel that comfortable, so I tried to swim back inside the reef.

But I was caught in what felt like a river of ocean water that was flowing from the shore out to sea. It was so strong that I would try to gain 15 feet then lose 20, gain 15 toward shore, then lose 20. I've been in rip tides and heavy waves before, but I've never felt anything like that.

I was breathing heavily and I realized that a snorkel doesn't provide enough oxygen to try to gasp through a tube. I tried to take my mask off just to gulp air, but the water was a little choppy so I was swallowing water at the same time.

I struggled against the current for about 15 minutes. I'm getting tired and I'm not getting enough air, so I start to call out for help, thinking I'd better do it earlier than later. I thought to myself, "I can't hold on too much longer."

Right at that moment, a wave picked me up and dumped me. It was so strong that it ripped off my fins. Without my fins, I'm without power and I'm feeling even more vulnerable. I was really exhausted by this time.

Then the thought came: "This is where I'm going to die. I'm going to die on Kauai. OK, there are worse places to die. I don't want to die, but I think this is where it's going to end because I don't think I can get out of this."

Dad, Hold On! I'm coming!

All of a sudden, I hear, "Dad, hold on! I'm coming!"

I was amazed to hear my son's voice. He was only about 10 or 15 feet away. I had not seen him coming toward me. Then he was right there next to me.

Taylor: While I had been on the sand, I saw my dad and he looked out way too far, and my mom and I were kind of worried. At first I thought we might be overreacting, but then I heard a faint distressed yell that convinced me that he needed help.

I ran to a pole that held a yellow foam floatation device called a Rescue Tube, unstrapped it from the Velcro, and stuffed a whistle that was there, too, in my bathing suit pocket. My mom anxiously told me not to go in and for a second I listened, but then I yelled, "Dad needs help!" I ran into the water yelling, "DAD!"

Once I swam past the reef and was in open water, my yells turned into high-pitched cracking screams as I swam desperately for him. A wave finally elevated me enough to see my dad. He was face down in the water with his snorkel and mask on. I don't think I will ever swim faster in my life. As I got to him he kept groaning and yelling "Oh, God!" I told him to grab onto the Rescue Tube and float on his back.

He did as I said, and he asked if I could put the Rescue Tube around my shoulder and swim back. I remembered the advice on the water safety video. I responded that the current was way too strong, and that someone was calling 911 and that they'd be here soon. Honestly, I wasn't sure if anyone was able to call 911. The beach was really remote and had no reception.

As we floated, I grabbed the whistle out of my pocket and blew as hard as I could every 20 seconds, to assure my mom that we hadn't drowned and to let people know where we were.

Kevin: Taylor was amazingly composed throughout this ordeal. At first I wasn't sure the Rescue Tube could hold us both, so I told him if it became difficult to stay afloat, that he should just let me go and I could periodically snorkel in the water nearby. He repeatedly told me, "I'm not going to let you go."

Taylor: I told my Dad that we just had to float, even if we were there for hours. I held his head up so he wouldn't inhale any more salt water. I told him when to hold his breath when a wave was coming, and

I also cupped my hand over his mouth to block the water.

My feeling that all we had to do was float and wait for a helicopter or Jet Ski died when my feet scraped an underwater rock. I tried to keep calm but I knew that I wanted to be in open water, not over a shallow reef where the waves could pound us at their will.

Just as I had that thought, I turned around to see a tall wave coming right for us. I screamed to my dad to hold his breath. The wave smashed us onto the reef. I was thrown and tumbled underwater, where I bounced on the reef and finally came up for air. The wave ripped my dad's mask and snorkel off his face, and we lost each other because he let go of the floatation device. Just when we thought we were okay, another wave smashed us against the reef again.

I knew this was not good for anyone's health. I tried to pick up my dad around his waist, but the reef was way too sharp on his knees and he couldn't walk.

Finally, I told my dad to lie down and grab onto the tube. I walked on the reef and pulled him back to the shore.

Kevin: Taylor hasn't said how much pain he was in. The rock ledge that he was walking on was full of shells and sharp rock. We had scrapes and scratches, he was bleeding on his feet, and he had to drag me. I commend him for enduring that pain to get us to shore.

Taylor: I knew that I was bleeding from the bottom of my feet but that wasn't what was on my mind. I had to get my dad back to shore.

I will never forget how selfless my dad was once we made it back to the sand. I asked one of the nude sunbathers for some water for my dad and my dad saved half of it for me. I couldn't convince him to drink any more until I did. He also was his gracious self, thanking the lifeguards who had just arrived and the man who had given us water.

Kevin: When we got back to the sand, I just kind of laid there. I remember saying something kind of sarcastic like, "That wasn't all that much fun." Then Taylor helped me to my feet and I felt fine at that point. We hiked back to the top of the cliff. I thought, "Let's just pack up and go home. I'm in need of a hot shower and a nap."

But fire and rescue teams were there at the top of the trail and they wanted to take me to the hospital. I thought, "I feel fine. I'm good, I'm good." They listened to my lungs and told me that I had water in my lungs, and that people have actually drowned from having water in their lungs days after surviving a situation like this. So they put an oxygen mask on me and we all went to the hospital.

I stayed in the hospital for a couple nights until their tests showed I was fine, and we flew home to California two days after the incident. All the rescue people involved at the scene and at the hospital were incredibly professional, calm, reassuring and competent.

So many times in life, the intervention of strangers makes a huge difference. I learned later that when it appeared I was in trouble, Su had tried to call 911, but the cliff and remote location of the beach prevented any phone connection. The man who had been the only other person swimming when I first went into the water, was the one who had run back up the steep trail to the parking area to get reception to call 911.

Maybe It was Fate

Su, Kevin's wife and Taylor's mother, is still in awe over her son's quick thinking that day and has shared their family's story with relatives and friends.

Su: We replay what happened at Larsen's Beach every day. Thanks to my son's heroic actions, and having a Rescue Tube on the beach, I did not return to Southern California as a widow, and my two sons still have a father.

Right after we got home, we would comment to each other about how amazing it was that if any one little factor had been different, it would have turned into a whole different story, like if Taylor hadn't seen the water safety video.

The Garvey family on Kauai several days before Kevin's near-drowning incident, from left, Su Choe-Garvey, Torrey, 8, Kevin, Taylor, 16. (Photo courtesy the Garvey family)

Taylor: I watched the water safety video in baggage claim at the airport and in a few other places. At baggage claim, I must've watched it five times; it was on a loop. Maybe it was fate or something telling me to watch it. I never thought in a million years that I would need that knowledge. I don't think anybody ever thinks that something like that is going to happen to them.

If that video had not been there, I probably would have just run out to my dad and we would have both been stuck in the middle of the ocean with nothing. It would have been two for one.

I decided I was in the best condition to save my dad. I wasn't going to have my mom or younger brother or anyone else do it. I'm glad that I made that decision.

Su: Taylor is very low-key about what he did that day. Once we got home, I told all my friends, but he didn't tell hardly anyone about what he did.

Taylor: Because you told everybody!

Su: We've found our family cause. We support Rescue Tubes in any way we can.

Kevin: After we got home to California, we were swimming in our pool one day. I said to Taylor, "You know, this doesn't mean I can't discipline you anymore, even though I owe you my life." He laughed and said, "I know, Dad."

Music on Kauai

Soundtrack of Our Lives

Music flows through Kauai life constantly as the soundtrack of our lives, describing moonlit nights, favorite island places and shared memories. Parties at beaches or in back yards naturally include music, friends bringing ukuleles or guitars for impromptu before-dinner jam sessions. In restaurants, when a musician plays a familiar song, an audience member may spontaneously dance hula. More than one island politician has been known to break into song at public events.

On Kauai, our musicians are ohana (*family*). We appreciate the pleasure their talents bring to our lives and they, in turn, appreciate our love of their art.

Slack Key Guitar

Stories tell us that Hawaiians probably learned to play guitar in the early-to-mid-1800s from Spanish cowboys who had been invited to Hawaii to help tame cattle. After a day's work, sitting around campfires, the Spaniards strummed guitars, one man playing melody, another playing the bass line, others playing background music.

When the Spaniards returned to Spain, they left some of their instruments behind. Hawaiians picked them up and learned to make the sounds of two or more guitars by using only one, developing a technique in which the thumb plays the bass line and the rest of the fingers play the melody. This intricate style of playing guitar became known as ki hoalu or slack key, and is a definitively Hawaiian form of music that is now known around the world.

Slack key is so named because the guitar strings are loosened or slackened, producing numerous tunings and the sweet tones that characterize ki hoalu. Under the nimble fingers of talented slack key artists, the lightly picked strings evoke sounds that stars would make if they could sing.

It's Got To Be Shared

Hal Kinnaman

Hal Kinnaman's whole being lights up when he talks about slack key guitar music, his youthful face looking like the enamored 26-year-old he was when he first heard the distinctive Hawaiian-style finger-picking guitar music being played on a Southern California beach more than 40 years ago.

A classically trained guitarist and instructor who studied in Spain and excelled in Flamenco and Bossa Nova, Hal tried to learn ki hoalu when he came to Hawaii, but was disappointed when a number of slack key experts told him they wanted to keep the knowledge within their own families. So Hal taught himself. He became a slack key master in his own right, sharing his knowledge at colleges on Oahu and Kauai, and through his easy-to-read instructional books, cassettes and CDs. In 1994, Hal was honored with the Folk Arts Apprenticeship Award from the Hawaii State Foundation on Culture and Arts for his work perpetuating the art of Hawaiian slack key guitar music.

Hal lives and breathes the musical life, the long fingernails on his right hand filed to points for ease in string-picking, Hawaiian words that describe music flowing effortlessly throughout his conversation. A warm friendly man, Hal's personality is as sweet as the ki hoalu melodies he plays, his blue eyes dancing as he talks about the happiness that sharing the art of Hawaiian slack key brings him.

From Your Heart

When I first heard slack key guitar being played, I had just gotten out of the water at a beach in Southern California and a Hawaiian man started playing it. I didn't know what it was but I just loved it. I said, "Wow, that's so soothing. That music is made for looking at and listening to the sounds of the ocean." The man, Ray Patterson, showed me some basics. I was already a classical guitar teacher, so it was easy for me to pick it up. Ray was always willing to share with me. We became affiliated with a hula halau (*hula school*) and performed up and down California. I dedicated my CD, "Revery," that I released in 2000 to Ray for our friendship and all he taught me.

I started coming to Hawaii in 1972 to learn more slack key guitar and to surf. Coming from a non-Hawaiian culture, I couldn't get in the door with a lot of people. Sometimes skilled players didn't want to share their family secrets of how to play. I saw that in Spain, too, with the Gypsies and Flamenco. I'd watch to learn how I could play it at home, but when they got to the good stuff, they'd turn away so I couldn't see what they were doing. That almost killed slack key. That's why a lot of us wrote methodologies and researched old songs before they got lost. If you don't share your art, you lose it. Thankfully, Raymond Kane on Oahu and a few other Hawaiian teachers shared enough with me so I could learn and teach others.

I wrote my first slack key instructional book called "Early Hawaiian Slack Key Melodies," in 1982 so people could learn to play their favorite songs on their own. At the time, only a few of us were writing musical tablature, showing the strings, frets and which fingers to use. I had the idea to include the rhythms, too: slide here, hammer here, pull it with your left hand, or add chimes or other vamps. I wrote "Teach Yourself Slack Key Guitar" in 1995 with the subtitle, "This easy-to-understand instructional booklet will have you playing in less time than you could imagine." I updated that into two booklets in 2012.

Slack key doesn't have to be intricate when you first start. It has to be nahenahe: sweet, gentle, flowing. It has to be puuwai, from your heart. When my students do all these things, it comes out beautifully: softly, slow it down, speed it up, tell a story. To students, all these things seem ridiculously hard at first, then all of a sudden they're inherently in their system. Pretty soon they're not thinking about them at all.

The old way of teaching is see, listen and imitate. I give students exercises. I show them how to put a chord down. I gleaned from all my guitar experience playing in string quartets, playing Mozart, Haydn, you name it, how to coordinate groups of muscles in your fingers. Sometimes it takes a student so long to put a chord down, the show's over and everybody's gone home. But with my exercises, I teach them how to put chords down fast. Then when you go to grab a chord, you have so much more coordination between the mind and the fingers.

If you're going to teach anything, you have to think from a beginner's perspective. You also have to know how the brain works. In my instructional books, I explain in words how to hold your hands on the guitar but some people are left brained, others are right brained. So I also had pictures drawn showing how to place your hand.

I love teaching for the joy of sharing and seeing people play when they didn't think they could do it. I had one student who was so shy, she couldn't even look up at me when she first started her lessons. Now she comes in and says, "Hi," sings and plays slack key.

One of the highlights of my life was being given the Folk Arts Apprenticeship Award from the Hawaii State Foundation on the

Culture and the Arts in 1994. I was totally blown away by that honor. It felt so good to get that recognition even though I wasn't Hawaiian.

Hal was one of the early performers who shared the art of slack key beyond Hawaii. A photo in his home shows him surrounded by Fijian children, their eyes looking at him and his guitar, entranced by the music.

I was one of the first to play in Fiji, giving free concerts in community centers. There was no electricity, thatched huts, only three cars on the island. One time the chief left me with the family and I was asked to read prayers in Fijian. It was sort of like Hawaiian, and of course they snickered at my pronunciation.

I was reminded while I was in Fiji how we all borrow musical phrases from our sisters and brothers and incorporate them into our songs. One night I was playing in a community center when the audience started clapping in the middle of my song. They were all excited. I thought, "What is that all about?" It turns out that a musical phrase in the song I was playing was a Fijian song. Music is all a mixture, a medley.

About nine years ago I started playing ukulele. I'd always heard that instrument just strummed and didn't know what else could be done on it. One of my students had been asking me for a month, "If you had a ukulele, what would you like?" I told him I'd want a wider neck because it's easier to put melody in.

One day the student showed up for his lesson with me and brought a beautiful tiger koa wood ukulele with tape across the top, above the tuning keys. He said, "Peel that tape off." I did, and there were my initials inlaid at the top of that ukulele in abalone shell! It had Spanish bracing and a wider neck than normal for my big hands.

My student made it himself. This is what instigated me to learn about ukulele.

Now I write music and change the tuning to the ukulele so that I can play slack key on it. I can retune it a different way to play Spanish classical music and I even play Bach on it! You're never going to get that wonderful bass sound because it's a higher-pitched instrument than a guitar, but by replacing the high string with a bass string that is an octave lower than on a normal ukulele, you get a more rich sound.

My favorite part of playing slack key has always been the relaxation. I play a lot of different musical styles and I always go to slack key to unwind. It makes you pono *(right)* in your life. It evens out the stress and helps you get back in balance.

You've got to have music. And it's got to be shared.

Music Shares Aloha
Paul Togioka

Kauai-born Paul Togioka is a slack key guitar master, subtly blending the traditional intricate finger-picking style with modern musical influences. Each of his compositions have a distinct sound and mood, both energizing and soothing at once. Recognized as one of Hawaii's best slack key artists, Paul has been awarded "Best Recording by a Slack Key Artist" and "Best Hawaiian Instrumental Recording" in the Hawaii Music Awards, and is also one of the performers on "Hawaiian Slack Key Kings" and "Hawaiian Slack Key Kings Volume II," both nominated for the national Grammy awards, the latter winning "Best Compilation Album" in the Na Hoku Hanohano Awards (Hawaiian Grammies).

Soft spoken and extremely humble, Paul, who was born to Japanese parents and raised in the sleepy town of Kekaha on Kauai's west side, talks about how he expresses himself through music and how performing slack key has opened doors for himself, while bringing enjoyment to others.

Music Sets the Mood

When I perform slack key, I am able to connect with people from all over the world. Visitors will come right up to me and say things like, "This is the best part of my vacation." It's a wonderful thing. Music shares aloha.

A good example is a celebrity wedding where I played guitar as background music. The wedding was held at a large hotel on Poipu Beach on Kauai's south shore. Security guards were there to keep uninvited guests out of the wedding. After the ceremony, the security guards left and I grabbed my ukulele and played more. Oh, then a big crowd came by. I thought people were just coming by to watch the sunset, but after I stopped playing, people on the balconies were clapping and other people came up to me and talked. I didn't even mean to do that. A man proposed to his girlfriend right there. The whole place started clapping for them. Maybe the music set the mood.

Full Blast into Slack Key

I got hooked on the guitar in my senior year in high school. You know how you see the surf and that's all you think about? That's how I was with guitar. That's all I thought about, 24/7.

I started off playing rock and roll stuff like Kansas, Boston, Led Zeppelin, the usual that young kids played. When I was in college at Colorado State University, I saw a guy playing a five-string banjo and took it up. That's a fast-paced, in-your-face instrument. I practiced so much for two years in Colorado, that when I came back to Kauai, I could play bluegrass music in the clubs. You can tell I wasn't studying much. I was just playing music.

One day I was in Kekaha, and I saw Isaac Kanahele *(a Niihau island native)* playing slack key. I was blown away by how one person could play the bass line and the melody at the same time. I stopped playing the electric guitar and I went full blast into slack key. I applied the banjo techniques I had learned to the guitar and I studied with Kauai master slack key instructor Hal Kinnaman over a couple year period to get my solid foundation.

One day my brother-in-law said a woman was looking for a musical soundtrack for something called the Kauai Talking Map. I told them that instead of paying me, I wanted the rights to my songs.

When we finished the project and I got the rights to the recordings, my brother-in-law said, "Why don't you make a CD?" I said, "No. What for? Who's going to buy it?" He kept encouraging me so I hired a steel guitar player and ukulele player and made a complete album. I played slack key on all the songs, but I was so shy back then, I didn't want to put my name out there. The CD cover says it was arranged by me and my friend Buddy Panoke.

I made 1,000 CDs and was going to give them away as Christmas gifts. Then a friend of mine said, "Why don't you send it in to the Hawaii Music Awards?" I did and I won "Best Recording by a Slack Key Artist."

Once that happened, the door opened. Milton Lau, a big producer from Honolulu, called me. He said, "I'd like you to perform at the Kauai slack key festival." I said, "Oh, wow, I would love to." Then he started naming some of the other artists who were going to perform: James "Bla" Pahinui, Martin Pahinui, Gary Haleamau, Brother Noland, Ledward Kaapana, Dennis Kamakahi, all the guys I really respected. I started getting all pressured out. I told him in the same phone call, "Maybe I shouldn't be doing this." He said, "I'll put you first." I was terrified. But I did it. It was good. I got to meet all the guys. They accepted me. There were no egos.

Then I came out with a second CD, and that won "Best Hawaiian Instrumental Recording" in the Hawaii Music Awards. Milton called me up and said he wanted to represent me, but he wanted me to go solo. I didn't want to do it. At that time I would surround myself on stage with a bunch of people because I didn't want to be on the stage alone. Milton actually flew to Kauai and stayed with me at my house to convince me to do it. As he left to go back to Oahu, he turned around and said to me, "You're going to know when you're ready."

It took seven years before I finally played solo at the slack key festival on Kauai. That night Milton called me up and offered me a recording deal. From that day on he took me on tour with him. I am grateful Milton believed in me. You need people like that who are willing to give you an opportunity.

Music is My Aloha

There are a lot of times I've doubted myself and said, "I'm going to quit." Because of the kind of personality I have, I worry a lot and expect a lot out of myself and I pressure myself out. I think part of it is from my upbringing. Because I came from an Oriental family, we tend to be shier and our parents tell us to be humble. And I came from a family that wasn't musicians. But then after this last slack key festival where I played solo, I said, "I cannot wait for next year!"

Eventually I started developing my own style. It's partly country and partly contemporary. I sometimes do songs that start off in the old style then morph into something modern. I feel that we've got to do the old style to remember our heritage but I don't believe you've got to do it all the time because everything changes.

New melodies just pop into my head. If I don't have a guitar with me when it happens, I call my home phone and hum it to my voice recorder. I weave Kauai into a lot of my songs. One day I was driving around and I heard a song in my head. I needed to get to my guitar so I could figure out the melody before I lost it. I pulled off into a parking lot at Kiahuna Plantation on the south shore. I called that song "Kiahuna Plantation Shuffle." "Kekaha Chimes" was a melody I came up with 10 years before I recorded it. I named it after my hometown.

I perform at as many as 200 events per year: weddings, blessings, parties and all kinds of private bookings. Sharing music is my aloha.

*Paul Togioka, left, and Hal Kinnaman, holding a ukulele,
are two of Kauai's most well-known slack key masters.
(Photo by Grant Honma)*

Kauai Brought Me Back to Music

Fran Kalb

Singer-songwriter Fran Kalb performed music on the mainland for years until her attention was diverted away from her natural talents for more than a decade. Upon moving to Kauai, she made connections that brought her back to her musical roots.

I believe that everything is all connected and that life comes full circle. Moving to Kauai has been that way for me.

I began writing songs when I was 13 years old with my sister. We wrote our own lyrics to other people's songs. An aspiring songwriter's got to start somewhere, right? My sister's birthday is March 26. You'll know why I'm telling you that in a moment.

Growing up, there was always music in the house, but it wasn't until I discovered a ukulele in the closet that had been my dad's from his Navy days that I first played an instrument. I opened the notebook that was with it and started teaching myself. Not long afterward I got my first guitar.

As I grew up and became an adult, I continued to write songs. In the mid- to late-1970s, a really good friend and I wrote a lot of music together and performed in cafes as a duo, playing guitar and singing our original songs. Her birthday was March 26, the same day as my sister's.

She and I recorded our first demo together, "Still Life," at a local recording studio. Music production was an adventure that I fell in love with. It's fun and exciting because you're taking your rough song and making a finished product. As other musicians and singers add their parts, it becomes a co-creation. It's the icing on the cake.

Life happens and my friend and I went our own ways, but I continued to write original songs. During the 1980s, I performed in several bands playing originals, jazz, Top 40 songs, rock and country. Musically it was a prolific and interesting time in my life.

In 1990 I started a business distributing health appliances internationally: juicers, dehydrators, those sorts of things. It was not creative or musical at all and I had to move to Los Angeles. The business took off and I did it for 14 yrs. During that time, I did some demos of some older music I had written, wrote a manuscript and did some screenplays. But my music largely went underground. It's ironic that I loved music, and here I was in this huge music center and was not engaged in music at all.

In 2003 my friend and I decided that it was time to get out of the rat race in L.A. and choose a different way of life. We came to Kauai for a visit and fell in love with the island and decided to move here. While I was tying up loose ends for the business and going back and forth between Los Angeles and Kauai, this same friend bought me a ukulele for my birthday. It was like coming home. I was inspired and started playing music again.

After I moved to Kauai, I got involved with a hula halau (*hula school*) where I was exposed to a lot of Hawaiian music. The melodies are so beautiful, and the lyrics honor nature and the world around us. The music sparked my creativity and I started writing songs again.

I said to myself, "I live somewhere that I love. I should be doing something that I love." Music has always been a passion of mine, and it's been there the whole time. Sometimes something's in front of your face and you never quite see it . . . until you're ready!

In 2007, I attended the Kauai Music Festival, a four-day conference where instructors, producers and other industry executives come to Kauai from all around the world to teach and discover new talent. I played one of my songs for one of the teachers, and he became my mentor.

In that moment, I made a commitment. I said, "I'm going to follow my heart and follow my dream because I really love this."

In December 2008, I went to a Christmas party and brought my ukulele. I played my song called, "Hawaiian Christmas Song." I also met Glenda and Dawna Delenstarr at that party.

About seven months later, at the next Kauai Music Festival, Glenda came up to me and said "Do you remember me from the party? You played that Christmas song. I'm a pianist and I have a piece of music that's an instrumental called 'Kauai Dream.' Would you write lyrics to it?" That was the beginning of our collaboration. And guess what? Her birthday is March 26!

Glenda and I recorded our first CD together, "Christmas From Hawaii," and on that CD is "Hawaiian Christmas Song," the very song I played at that party where I met her. In 2012 our CD was nominated for a Na Hoku Hanohano Award. Those are like the Grammy Awards of Hawaii.

In 2014, I started my own record label, NuArt Records, released my first single, "Rockin' on Jupiter," and also produced my first music video for that song. I love the process of writing and producing a song and the final result is always exciting. I'm also happy to be working with and mentoring some very talented local artists.

Kauai has been a very magical place for me. It's brought me back home to the realization that we all have some gift, something that we are here to share with other people. For me, it is music.

From where I stand, Heaven is all around me
With every breath, living aloha.

— From "Living Aloha"
©Fran Kalb

Hiking Kauai

Hiking Kauai

Hikers of all skill levels are enticed by Kauai's mountain ranges that beckon with lush green valleys carved by eons of weathering, rising to peaks that promise breathtaking views from their summits. Trails range from easy, scenic strolls on country paths to rigorous treks across unforgiving terrain.

One of Kauai's most popular hiking destinations is the Kalalau Trail along the Napali Coast on the island's northwest shore, a narrow footpath that winds across cliff faces hundreds of feet above crashing surf below, on the way to serene Kalalau Valley. People come from around the world to experience this challenging 11-mile trail that begins at Kee Beach where the highway ends on the north shore. Each day hikers make the four-mile roundtrip to and from the first beach, Hanakapiai. Beyond, the trail becomes more demanding and is only for those who are skilled and hardy.

Hikers are also attracted to Mount Waialeale, an extinct volcano at the center of the island that is known as "The Wettest Spot on Earth" for the 400 to 600 inches of rain it receives each year. Waialeale, and the highest peak in the Waialeale range, Kawaikini, nearly one mile above sea level, are frequently shrouded in clouds. When visible from below, they resemble a masterpiece painting, scores of white-ribboned waterfalls streaming down from above.

Come along with four Kauai people as they relive their adventures exploring the nearly-private beach of Kipu Kai, Kalalau Valley, hiking along the Napali Coast and climbing Mount Waialeale.

Hikers traverse the first two miles of the Kalalau Trail,
before the trail narrows.
(Photo by Pamela Varma Brown)

Kipu Kai Memories
By Ray Smith

Ray Smith recalls visiting Kipu Kai, a gem of a valley and near-ly-private beach on Kauai's southeast shore that is accessible only by ocean, or by permission of the owners of the valley.

Ray grew up on Kauai in the 1940s and graduated from Kauai High School, where he was sports editor of both the school's newspaper and yearbook. He began writing for The Garden Island, Kauai's daily newspaper, at age 16, covering the barefoot football team Koloa Pa-lutes, launching a 55-year career in print journalism that took him to more than 35 countries. Ray now lives in Wheaton, IL and returns to Kauai often, more than 35 times so far.

I had the thrill of hiking into the pristine, remote and private-ly-owned Kipu Kai valley twice as a boy. For decades, the main trail was a Hawaiian-era stone path through the cut beneath the towering 2,300-foot Mount Haupu in the majestic Hoary Head mountain range. Several memorable episodes about Kipu Kai remain etched in my mind.

In the summer of 1943 during World War II, Dr. Albert Herbert Waterhouse, a cousin of the owner of Kipu Kai, escorted a hiking party of a handful of adults and 11-year-old me into the valley where we picnicked, swam and admired the peacocks roaming wild.

Two years later, in the summer of 1945, the good doctor took three other adults and me, back in from the Koloa side of Kipu. We drove the two miles through cane fields, parked under an ironwood tree at Mahaleupu and squeezed through a tiny break in the fence at the base of what locals call Black Mountain, hiked up the ridge and bushwhacked our way down into the valley.

We began exploring the verdant valley, careful to steer clear of wild peacocks and roaming cattle. After skinny-dipping in the calm cove in the lee of Molehu Point, we sat on the porch of the owner's unoccupied cottage — Doc had a key — eating our lunches.

After lunch I wandered away and, noticing it was possible to edge on the rocks between incoming waves around the north cliff face toward Nawiliwili, I crept, barefoot, of course, into the next valley. Hokonu is one-third the size of Kipu Kai, totally untouched, accessible only by sea. Walking some 50 yards along the beach I spotted something sticking out of a sand dune and pulled out a skull. Looking around to see if there was a kahuna (*Hawaiian priest*) lurking, I quickly reburied it. A year earlier I had taken a Hawaiian skull home from near Poipu, though my mother somehow disposed of it.

As our group headed back mid-afternoon, strolling down the length of Long Beach, my Uncle John hollered, "Look!" He pointed to an object being washed in by the waves about 15 yards out in the water. It was a huge glass ball about 18 inches wide. When we got to the very end of the beach, we saw dozens of glass balls of all sizes, round and elongated, in various shades of green and purple, washed up above the tide line. These prized souvenirs had broken loose from fishing nets from Japan, with whom the U.S. was still at war, and floated on currents to this remote beach on Kauai. Creating bags from our T-shirts, everyone hauled home as many as we could carry, reluctantly leaving almost half still lying there.

More than 65 years later, I still have one five-inch round ball that still has salt water with tiny particles trapped inside. The water must have been forced in through invisible pukas (*holes*) in the glass from the pressure of being submerged in the deep ocean while attached to a Japanese fishing net.

When I returned to Kauai in 1963 after a 13-year absence, I took off one morning to scale Kawelikoa Peak along the Haupu ridgeline, a sheer drop to the ocean. There was no trail as I climbed over the barbed wire fence and beat my way through lantana up the hillside, then pulled myself hand-over-hand up the final rocky ridge.

I found two surprises at the level top: a geodesic marker placed in 1933 by the Department of Interior indicating we were 733 feet above sea level; and barbed wire evidence that back in 1942 there had been a manned U.S. Army observation post up there. Talk about lonely duty! I suspect that post was created after Kauai was shelled in January 1942 by a Japanese submarine that lobbed several shells at night intending to hit harbor installations, but that overshot into Grove Farm's cane fields, starting a small fire that was extinguished.

Twenty years later I hiked into Kipu Kai again, careful not to be spotted. I hope the statute of limitations for trespassing has expired! This time I went all the way down to the beach just to see if there were any glass balls, but auwe (*alas*), no more. About 10 years ago I went up again and took some spectacular pictures from the top.

Seven decades since my first hike into Kipu Valley, a half dozen glass balls in a monkeypod wood bowl in our den remain my reminders of some very special times at Kipu Kai.

The Splendor of Kalalau Valley
By Gabriela Taylor

Gabriela Taylor first hiked the rugged 11-mile Kalalau Trail along the Napali Coast into Kalalau Valley in 1972, fell in love with Kauai, and moved to the island the following year. She has hiked into the valley almost annually since then. Here she shares her experiences traversing the narrow footpath, and the joy, beauty and pure relaxation of the secluded, pristine valley.

Kalalau Valley and the entire Napali Coast is the most awe-inspiring place I've ever hiked, and I've hiked all over the world: the Andes, the Himalayas, the Rockies, New Zealand, Africa, Indonesia, China. Views are spectacular: when you gaze out from the trail, you can actually see the curve of the Earth on the horizon, while down below, powerful waves crash against the lava cliffs. The night sky transforms into an expansive canopy of brilliant stars in Kalalau, where stunning sunsets and falling stars provide entertainment for campers. It's a mystical place where tranquility and peace embrace me.

Hiking to Kalalau is a pilgrimage for me, an arduous trek in which the journey is as important as the destination. It challenges me as the red dirt trail ascends from sea level to several hundred feet, drops down again and again, and snakes into and out of emerald green hanging valleys where breathtaking waterfalls seem to pour down from the heavens. In some areas, you're lucky if there are rocks to provide footing across gushing streams. On these hikes, I'm reminded how powerfully Mother Nature rules. If you don't show respect or pay attention to her, you can have any number of unpleasant surprises: rock falls, twisted ankles, slip-and-falls and drownings are not uncommon on the trail or in Kalalau Valley. When needed, a HELP sign is carved onto the beach sand to alert a passing helicopter for emergency evacuation. Cell phones don't work in the remoteness of the Napali Coast.

The first time I hiked to Kalalau was in 1972 after one of my students raved about her experience there. Being a novice, I carried a pack that was much too heavy. Before my friend and I even got to the stream upon entering Kalalau Valley, we were so exhausted that we lay down on the ground and slept, not even in a campground, awakening in the middle of the night to find ourselves surrounded by cattle just staring down at us. After that I learned to carry a much lighter pack with dried food and to forage for mangoes, lilikoi (*passion fruit*) or whatever is in season, catch opae (*fresh water shrimp*) with a small net and to harvest watercress in the stream. In the past few years, I camped with friends who are gourmet cooks and who brought all sorts of elaborate food. While it was delicious, truthfully, it wasn't any more satisfying than eating a simple meal, since everything is tasty when you're camping.

When I'm at Kalalau, it feels as though I'm in a dream world, in a fantasyland that is even more beautiful than I could imagine. That's what has always drawn me back: no roads, no cars, no telephones or computers. People go there to hear the peaceful sounds of nature, though sometimes they bring musical instruments like flutes or guitars and play around a campfire in the evening.

My favorite camping spot is among trees overlooking the beach, only steps away from my "shower," a 60-foot high, two-tiered waterfall where people bathe as well as fill water bottles. It provides a deep tissue massage, penetrating the sore spots. You don't have any choice but to relax; pure mountain water cleanses both literally and symbolically, removing remnants of regular life.

After a strenuous eight-hour hike into Kalalau, I typically relax the next day by taking a half-hour walk to the stream where I treat myself to a Jacuzzi. Step one: Find a comfortable sitting position under a small waterfall, then let the water pound over tight shoulders and back. Of course, the effect is far superior without clothing. Step two: Locate a large rock, climb on and dry off in the sun. Once, just as I settled down on the warm rock, I turned my head toward the mouth of the stream where fresh water meets the azure blue ocean only about 50 feet away. I was jolted out of my reverie by the sight of a gigantic white cruise ship passing ever so slowly just offshore, right in front of the stream. It looked like a mirage as cameras flashed from figures lining the decks of the ship. Of course, they were taking photographs of Kalalau Valley, but I wondered if any passengers were surprised later upon discovering a mermaid perched on a rock in the foreground of their picture.

Everything about Kalalau Valley is big, bold and dramatic. Monstrous surf will pound cliffs in winter and fill caves with saltwater, completely wiping out any trace of human existence. I like to swim and body surf when the ocean is not too rough, normally in summer. Walking along the beach, I pass gigantic sea caves that serve as shelter for dozens of campers who set up tents or just sleep on the sand. In contrast to the towering mountains and vast seascape, their bright yellow and red kayaks look like toys forgotten on the beach.

The wet cave, a 10-minute stroll past the camping caves, is pure intrigue for me. I call it "the castle," because rock ramparts crown its towering cliffs, while a pool of fresh water down below serves as a moat that must be crossed to enter. Mountain rain filters through the cave roof to create a pool that extends at least 90 feet back inside. Four feet at the deepest point, one can swim or walk in through this enchanted kingdom where water reflects moving patterns of light on the cave's rough black and red lava walls. The only sound is water flowing around your body and sometimes that of swooping, screeching birds. A sandy beach resides at the back of the dimly-lit cave from where one can view only a small hole of light framed by the cave entrance, and listen to the muffled pounding of surf. So far away from anything familiar, for me, it is truly a sacred experience to be standing under a huge lava mountain and to feel totally safe and nurtured.

When I mention Kalalau to most people, they want to tell their story about the trail or the valley. But I'm most intrigued by the many stories that can no longer be told. Native Hawaiians who inhabited Kalalau Valley for hundreds of years left behind stone-walled taro terraces and sacred ritual grounds called heiau (*ancient Hawaiian places of worship*). The jungle devoured their structures and artifacts, made from natural materials. Their stories remain with ghosts of bygone years whose spirits are said to inhabit the valley.

Now, state-issued camping permits allow time to explore Kalalau Valley with all her pools, waterfalls and maybe even wild mangoes. Being there is like returning to childhood — running free and happy. It is also about slowing down, being still and meditative as is experienced during sunset. Heeding Mother Nature's clock, campers emerge out of the trees well before the sun sets, sit on the beach and silently wait. If it is a Kalalau extravaganza, we stare at the brilliant reds, oranges and yellows of an outrageous sky, and if luck has it and we don't blink, we'll see a green flash, momentarily, just as the shining ball of light sinks below the horizon.

Millions of twinkling stars emerge from the inky black sky at night as I lie on the sand in my sleeping bag, immersed in the vastness of eternity. After an hour, a searchlight appears way out in the ocean and moves slowly toward the shore. It's the full moonlight breaking over the pali (*cliff*), but the moon itself won't be overhead for another hour. I give thanks, close my eyes and dream that I'm being bathed in moonlight in a magical place called Kalalau.

Surviving A Storm On the Kalalau Trail

By Gabriela Taylor

Gabriela Taylor has hiked the Kalalau Trail almost annually since 1972. Here she shares a story of the perils of this trail and the power of Mother Nature.

As I am leaving Kalalau Valley after camping here for four days, I turn back and gaze down from the top of Red Hill as late afternoon sunlight illuminates vertical edges of the valley's green folds, intensifying the wonderment of this magical place. Taking in the white strip of beach where I camped with friends, I give thanks, then turn to continue the five-mile hike to Hanakoa Valley where I will spend the night.

I have hiked the Kalalau Trail almost yearly since 1972, and it has always been an opportunity for spiritual renewal for me, a journey where challenge as well as awe only enhances the quality of the quest. I enjoy making the trek alone because I can totally immerse myself in the natural world.

However, one thing concerns me today. Although the day has been sunny and the trail is perfectly dry, I notice an indigo-colored cloud hanging ominously in the sky up ahead. After a half hour of hiking, I encounter a young couple from Spain, wet clothing plastered against their bodies. Fifteen minutes later, two hardy looking Germans walk past, complaining about the slipperiness of the wet trail behind them. Should I go back and hike out tomorrow? "No," I tell myself. "Right now I have the momentum and the will to continue despite the odds of difficulty ahead." After all, I've frequently hiked this challenging 11-mile trail under difficult circumstances, including when a section of the trail around the eight-mile mark was so eroded that hikers had no option but to crawl along a cliff known as "Crawler's Ledge" that dropped hundreds of feet to the pounding surf below.

Traversing switchbacks through a handful of small valleys, I recognize favorite landmarks, including a waterfall and pool where I bathed on my way into the valley. No time to jump in the pool now as I climb up out of the protected forest and head toward the cliff face overhanging the ocean. Little do I know that I will face the greatest challenge of all my decades of hiking just a few dozen strides ahead.

Rounding the bend, I am blasted by the brunt of a storm, wind and driving rain assaulting me. I begin reciting affirmations while proceeding cautiously along the narrow, slippery ledges. "I am strong and as sure-footed as a goat. My shoes cling to the trail like gecko feet," I proclaim loudly while placing one foot firmly in front of the other onto the foot-wide path, as well as when I'm forced to leap over a gully where the trail has completely caved in. I feel like an aerialist balancing on a wire because there is no vegetation to grab onto for security, only the occasional protruding rock that serves as a handhold, or more precisely, a lifeline. Leaning into the orange dirt cliff, I never look to the left over the edge where raging surf crashes against black lava rocks far below. But just knowing about that potential peril turns my legs rubbery. Fear grips me when I think, "If I fall, there will be no one to witness it. I will disappear into the ocean below." Only now does solo hiking seem foolhardy.

Pulling myself together, I begin chanting familiar phrases from my spiritual practice and carefully watch every step as I begin breathing rhythmically. Then something shifts deep within me. Every body part awakens; animal-like, muscles, skin, eyes, nose and ears attune to nature. As I proceed mindfully along the cliffs now, I feel as exhilarated as I do when body-surfing or dancing wildly to a drumbeat. I pass the last treacherous ledge and begin my zigzag ascent up Century Plant Hill. Twenty–foot tall stalks marching along the slope seem to welcome me as I gratefully hold onto them for security and acknowledge that this will be the last quarter-mile before descending into Hanakoa Valley. I look up to see a pastel rainbow arching over the rainforest, a welcome mat, an affirmation to my survival and a congratulatory message heralding, "You have made it!"

I plan to sleep in the first shelter, but can see right away that it's filled with soaked tents and bulging with bodies. I trudge off toward the second shelter and discover that the stream is too big and dangerous to traverse at the regular crossing. Playing it safe, I hike 10 minutes up stream and find a relatively calm place to cross. Relieved, I walk toward the shelter, but am taken by surprise to see a Hawaiian woman's face peering out through the semi-dark rain ahead and worry that this shelter may also be full. Strangely, upon reaching the shelter, no one is there. Hanakoa Valley, once inhabited by Hawaiians, is reportedly filled with spirits whom I've always considered to be friendly ghosts. This time I'm sure of it.

Hungry and exhausted, I consume trail mix and dried apricots as though they're gourmet treats, strip off soaked clothing, zip myself into a sleeping bag, and settle in for the night on top of a picnic table. Torrents of rain pound like tiny mallets on the metal roof above the table, the nearby river roars, and millions of raindrops hit myriad leaves like percussion instruments in a rocking jungle jam session. No matter the racket, I am warm and happy in Hanakoa Valley, the wettest spot on Kauai's entire coast, and give thanks to all the Hawaiian spirits with whom I will spend the night as I doze off.

After a deep night's sleep, I open my eyes the next morning to sparkling sunshine and feel absolutely ecstatic. I acknowledge that my frightening experience of the day before, no matter how painful it seemed at the time, was a gift that led to my present feeling of renewal, as well as gratitude for my entire life.

Unforgettable Hike
By Cara Kruse

Cara Kruse's first-ever hike ever was on Mount Waialeale when she was 13 years old. Three years later, Cara looks back at her adventures on that wonderful day traversing the extinct volcano located in the center of Kauai.

One day my brother, Cameron, who is 12 years older than I am, said, "We're going on a hike." It was my first hike. I was excited to do it. I'd seen stuff like that on TV.

I didn't know where we were going until he and I and his girlfriend, Rachel, were in the truck and he said we were going to hike Mount Waialeale. I knew it was the wettest place on Earth and I knew it had giant waterfalls. I hadn't really pictured it as a hiking spot. I thought, "We'll see how this goes."

We arrived at the base of the mountain to begin our hike around 1 p.m. As I stood there, I thought about how Mount Waialeale had always seemed insurmountable to me, but as we climbed, I was struck by the mountain's grand beauty, picturesque waterfalls and towering greenery.

We began at a steady pace up a dirt trail, which soon conjoined with a forest of trees, overgrown brush and mud. Soon we found ourselves in a swampy area where it felt like we were in another forest. It looked like an entirely different place than where we started.

I felt like I was in quicksand at one point because my shoe got stuck in the mud.

The hike was a combination of maze-like trails and tedious climbing over rocks alongside streams. Some rocks were as big as three feet and we had to hold onto their sides to climb over them. I thought we might get lost, but Rachel, who was quite the mountaineer, led the way. Traces of sunlight were infrequent through the forest canopy, and we heard the sound of rushing waterfalls the closer we got to the top of Waialeale.

We had to cross over the top of waterfalls twice. One time Cameron had to carry both Rachel and me over one. I was sort of scared because it was flowing pretty fast. Fortunately he's 6-foot-4.

The time seemed to fly by. I don't know how much ground we covered but it seemed like a lot. We only stopped a couple times for water and snacks.

After we climbed for five hours, we could see our destination, which was the top of the mountain, but by then it was 6 p.m. With an unclear path and conscious of time ticking away, we decided to head back down the mountain. We got back to our truck at 9 p.m.

Even though we didn't make our goal of reaching the top of Waialeale, we were elated. Sure, we were hungry and thirsty, but we had accomplished an eight-hour hike filled with perfect amounts of challenge, trust, scenery and mud painting our clothing. My first hike was incomparable and I'll remember it for the rest of my life. I hope to one day return to the astounding Mount Waialeale and reach the top.

Mount Waialeale, the extinct volcano from which Kauai was created,
filled with waterfalls after a passing tropical storm.
Top left, a rare sight of Kawaikini, at 5,243 feet, the tallest peak in the
Waialeale range, normally shrouded in clouds.
(Photo by Pamela Varma Brown)

Two Nights Atop
Mount Waialeale
By David O'Quinn

David O'Quinn is a massage therapist who has lived on Kauai since 1989. Six times he had hiked to Blue Hole, a stunning location at the base of the waterfalls that flow down the face of Mount Waialeale —until the following adventure, during which he spent two nights in one of the rainiest spots on Earth.

In January 2006 I was preparing to leave Kauai for a new life of traveling the globe to visit sacred sites. Before I left, I wanted to visit my beloved Mount Waialeale. This crater of an ancient volcano has always felt like the birthplace of my soul on this planet. The weather that winter had been dry and sunny, excellent conditions for hiking the "Wettest Spot on Earth."

My first mistake was to go alone. I chose to do so rather stubbornly because every time I have gone with another hiker, they have never wanted to complete the trip. This time I was determined to go as far as the trail would allow.

I packed a very light backpack consisting of two quarts of water, a small bag of trail mix, one lightweight beach towel, two crystals and a small flashlight, and set out for Blue Hole, located at the base of the mountain.

I began at 10 a.m., reaching the first large waterfall in two-and-a-half hours, a hike that had taken me four hours on past trips. I climbed the rocks along the waterfall and followed the narrow path as far as I could go and came to a large pool fed by a short waterfall. I knew this was not the Blue Hole, but I could not find the trail that would take me to the end. I did, however, find a magical spot in what looked like a fairy glen surrounded by moss-covered trees, back-dropped by three cascading waterfalls that flowed some 3,000 feet. I sat and meditated at the spot.

It was now almost 3 p.m. and I wanted to return before dark. Around 4:30 p.m., I was about 30 minutes from completing my trek, but my body and feet were exhausted from endlessly scaling boulders. As I approached the crossing of the last feeder stream, the trail seemed to disappear. In my haste I chose a wrong stream fork to follow and came to a sheer, steep waterfall, that fortunately was very light, but there was no way around it. It was 6 p.m., almost dark and I was not sure what to do. I knew I was lost.

I made a near fatal decision and chose to climb up the cliff side. My logic told me that if I scaled the cliff I would end up on the road near where I had parked my truck.

The hillside was sheer, wet and crumbly. Vines and ferns were so thick that they seemed determined to block my ascent. I swore as thorns tore at my legs, hands and arms, but I soon forgave them because at times they were all I had to hold onto. It soon became very dark with the exception of a fine haze of moonlight.

My climb up the cliff face took five-and-a-half hours. For every foot I gained, I sometimes fell 10 feet, but fortunately did not injure myself badly. I finally pulled myself over the edge into the moonlight and was able to rest at the top. It was 10:30 p.m. The good news was that I lived to write this. The bad news was that the road I thought I was going to find was not there. I had absolutely no idea where I was.

I didn't have enough strength to go farther, so I chose a spot under a stubby tree near some shrubs. The rain came along with wind. It was cold and I had not prepared myself to stay the night. I couldn't remember being this cold since the first time I went camping with the Boy Scouts on a frosty night in February too many years ago.

I was also angry with myself for how I had spent the past month. I had focused almost entirely on preparing to leave Kauai and had spent so little time with my friends and loved ones, that I wondered if they knew how much they meant to me. I was awake all night pondering these thoughts.

When dawn arrived, one thing became apparent: if I had been able to see where I was going the night before I would have never taken the route I did. I found myself higher than many of the surrounding peaks. I could not see over the side to determine how I would climb down. I envisioned flagging down one of the many helicopters that came through these passages on sightseeing tours.

Climbing a tree, I waved my towel desperately at the passing helicopters but they could not see me. One chopper took a short cut and came so close to me that I fell over backward in tall ferns to keep from being hit, but to my surprise, he did not see me either. By 9:30 that morning, one tour helicopter acknowledged me by circling. Hope warmed my veins and I thought surely this would be over soon. Two hours later, a small helicopter from the Pacific Missile Range Facility on Kauai's west side flew by, saw me and circled. Hovering overhead, one of the men leaned out of the open side door. "Hallelujah," I thought. "I am going home!" After a short pause, to my surprise, they closed the door and took off. My spirits dropped.

By 3 p.m. I had flagged down a couple of other tour helicopters, including the first one that had seen me, as he flew over with a new group of passengers. Each pilot acknowledged me but no one actually stopped. Perhaps they thought that because I had been able to stand up and wave that I was OK and did not need help.

Fog blanketed the area again and more rain fell. I had run out of water to drink. My body was starting to show signs of hypothermia. My hands alternated between numbness and pain. My extremities were turning blue and I was experiencing muscle cramping in my abdomen. I was not sure my body would make it another night.

I laughed at the irony of my situation. Perhaps none of this was by accident, even all the bad choices I had made. Could it be this was my time to die? If so I picked a beautiful resting place.

Around 5 p.m., I heard a loud voice in my head that said, "Get up David O'Quinn. It is not your time to die. Keep trying to get the attention of helicopters until they stop searching." I also heard other voices. I was not sure if someone was calling for me or they were lost themselves. I yelled back, "Are you lost? Do you need help?" I could not understand their reply, but I learned later that a party of hunters had come looking for me. I spent another sleepless night on the top of Waialeale.

If there was one surprise in all of this, it was that I felt as though I had approached death as a coward. I had always believed that I would be spiritually smug in the face of death. I believed death was just a transition from one type of life to another. But the first night I spent much time in cathartic releasing both in tears and verbal beseeching. By the second night on this mountain peak, I was in such a place of surrender that I didn't care that it stormed all night, and I had stopped checking my watch to see what time it was.

The next morning, the mountain was ensconced in thick fog. Rescue helicopters started flying around 7 a.m. but they were looking much lower on the mountain than where I was, and they could not hear my shouting. By 9 a.m. I gave up trying to get anyone's attention, and sat under my towel trying to block the wind and showers. I learned a new appreciation for my body's resilience.

A half hour later, I heard another strong inner voice instructing me to get up and go where I had been the day before, that the fog would lift briefly and a helicopter would spot me. I did so, and to my surprise, I was treated to a spectacular display of waterfalls.

Just then, a helicopter pilot who had spotted me the day before, flew overhead twice. Another chopper moved in and hovered overhead. A man leaned out of the second helicopter and called to me through a megaphone but I indicated that I could not hear him. The pilot kept circling until a Navy rescue helicopter arrived. To my relief, a Navy man lowered down a basket that landed on the ferns beside me. The ferns were almost as tall as I, and this basket was small with no straps. As I dropped into the basket, it began to tumble over the hillside. If you happened to have caught my rescue on the television news, they did not include that bit of footage. I held on tightly until they started hoisting me up. Once in the helicopter it was not long before they got me to Lihue Airport where an ambulance was waiting to take me to Wilcox Memorial Hospital.

Six hours and four bags of IV fluid later, I was able to see the sun again.

My physical scars healed very quickly, thanks to the love, remedies and energy given to me from my wonderful friends, but it was some months before the emotional scars went away.

I gained a new sense of courage from this experience. Now, whenever I experience a situation that feels overwhelming or unknown, I remember being cold, wet, tired and unsure if I would survive my hike on Mount Waialeale, and whatever challenge I am facing becomes insignificant.

Wayfinding

Wayfinding

For centuries, Kauai people have heard stories about their Polynesian ancestors sailing thousands of miles across the Pacific Ocean in voyaging canoes, discovering and exploring distant lands.

In 1975, modern voyagers began recreating these adventures aboard Hokulea, a handsome 62-foot long double-hulled, twin-masted canoe built as a working replica of ancient Polynesian sailing vessels. In Hawaiian, her name means "Star of Gladness."

Hokulea is navigated using only the same tools that Polynesians had available 1,500 years ago: the stars and planets, sun, moon, wind, ocean swells, cloud formations, patterns of migratory birds and other forms of natural guidance. Collectively, these navigation methods are called "wayfinding." No modern implements are allowed on Hokulea, except a radio for safety purposes. No GPS, no maps, not even watches.

Hokulea and her many Hawaiian crews have traveled the equivalent of six times around the earth, visiting numerous countries including New Zealand, Tahiti, Palmyra, Micronesia, Canada and Japan. Everywhere the canoe has journeyed, she and her sailors have been received as symbols of peace, hope, compassion and of the promise that humankind can live in harmony with nature and with each other.

Here are the stories of three of Kauai's modern adventurers who have sailed on Hokulea. They share their experiences of wayfinding Polynesian-style, and how it changed their lives.

"Full Moon of Kauai" by scratchboard artist Michelle Dick: a voyaging canoe sailing along the cliffs of Kauai's Napali Coast.
(Courtesy Michelle Dick)

Feel the Canoe

Dennis Chun

Dennis Chun is one of Kauai's pioneers in Polynesian-style voyaging. He's an icon among younger sailors and students who learn about his journeys aboard Hokulea, including when he traveled from Hawaii to Tahiti twice; from Hawaii to the Marquesas Islands; in Japan from Fukuoka to Oshima and Uwajima; and from Rapa Nui (Easter Island) to Tahiti.

A professor of Hawaiian Studies and Culture at University of Hawaii's Kauai Community College, Dennis is extremely humble, always deflecting honor to others. Looking as youthful as when he first walked aboard Hoku, as he affectionately calls the large canoe, and speaking by turns scholarly and playfully, Dennis reflects on the fun and life-changing experiences he has had while sailing Polynesian-style.

I was there for the launching of Hokulea in March 1975 on Oahu when I was a student at University of Hawaii at Manoa. When I saw it, I wanted to be on it. It just kind of slid into the water. It looked like it was going to take off. That was real chicken-skin (*goose bump*) time.

I first sailed Hoku in 1976. I was a young squirt, just a crew guy, whatever needed to be done. There were more experienced sailors. In the beginning, we sailed around Oahu. It was only when we began sailing between the islands overnight that I started to understand what it was like for the ancestors. We didn't have a nice warm cabin

Hokulea in full sail.
(Drawing by Keala Kai)

to jump in and no compass.

When we sailed to the South Pacific, I thought it was going to be like in the movies: sunny, warm. Reality was a lot different. The first night, I froze my butt off. I said, "This is cold, man!" I thought back to the ancient Polynesian voyagers and said, "Damn, how did those guys do it?" No foul weather gear. We tried wearing malos (*loincloths*) all the time. In the daytime, it was fine. When nighttime came, I put on my Patagonia sweatpants!

Our first navigator of Hokulea was Nainoa Thompson whose teacher was Mau Piailug, a master navigator from the tiny Micronesian coral atoll of Satawal that is only about half a square mile in size. Mau learned wayfinding methods from his grandfather who taught him to observe wind patterns and changes in ocean swells when they paddled out in a canoe. As Mau got older, he sailed every day, gradually venturing farther and farther from his home atoll. He learned to understand patterns and signs everywhere. In that kind of lifestyle, you become more observant because your life depends on it: when it's good to go fishing; when you're not going fishing; when you need to tie down your canoes; when you need to tie down your sail, because that cloud over there means the wind will be too strong for this canoe.

Mau taught us to sail by observing everything around us. He had this sixth sense of what's happening, and he wanted us to learn how to feel things. After the movie "Star Wars" came out, we used to call him Yoda, after the Jedi master who could predict the future.

One of my best memories was when we were sailing Hokulea from Hawaii to Tahiti in 1985. I was just getting into the understanding of how wayfinding works. Mau's bunk was next to where I was steering. He used to reach his arm out and pull my leg if there was something I should know. He'd say, in his Micronesian-accented broken English, "Dennis, you steering too low. Bring the canoe up." I wondered how he could tell. He could feel it even when he was sitting in the hull, just a sixth sense. He'd say, "Feel the canoe, feel the canoe." After awhile, you'd kind of get into it.

One night, after it had been raining for four or five days, we were wet and miserable. It's about 11 p.m. or midnight. It's cold. Mau's sitting in his compartment, I'm steering. Mau pulls my leg.

I say, "Yeah, Mau, am I off?"

"No, no. You good."

He hands me a coconut cup with liquid inside.

"Here, drink for you."

"No, I'm not thirsty."

"No, it's good for you."

So I picked it up, brought it to my nose and hooo! It was one whole cup of Crown Royal!

"Mau, we're not supposed to be having alcohol onboard."

"Drink, you feel better."

Later, the same night while I was still steering, Mau asked, "Dennis, plenty rain, yeah? You like rain stop? Tomorrow, I make magic. Rain stop." I said, "Yes, Mau. I would like you to make the rain stop."

I finished my shift and went to bed. Usually when it's raining there's no levity. I woke up around 2 a.m. to the sound of laughing, people talking story. I opened my eyes, unzipped my compartment flap, stuck my head out. The sky's clear, not raining and everyone's got their clothes out on the railing drying. Mau looks at me, smiles and says, "Oh, Dennis, you like?"

How did Mau stop the rain? He said, "I sing certain song." I think it's more intuition. He can feel certain changes, certain things going on in the environment. These are the kinds of things he wanted to us to learn.

Guidance Appears in Many Forms

Using only nature's guidance when sailing can present certain challenges when those clues are temporarily unavailable, such as during cloudy nights or heavy rainstorms. On the 9,500-mile journey from

Hawaii to the Marquesas in 1995, Hokulea skimmed along the ocean, making good time toward the cluster of small islands in the southern Pacific Ocean. Then one night the wind suddenly died. As canoe and crew bobbed around in the doldrums, day became night, the sky became cloudy, hiding the stars and planets, making it impossible for the captain to see which way to go. Rain squalls moved in, soaking the crew. The next day, more of the same. As darkness fell into night once more, the overcast sky remained solid. That's when Dennis and the rest of the Hokulea crew learned that guidance appears in many forms.

I was on the second watch, from about 9 or 10 p.m. to 2 or 3 a.m. We couldn't see anything to navigate by. You've just got to go by ocean swells to get the feel of how the boat feels on the waves.

Then we start hearing a sound. Psshhhhh. Whshhhh. It was a pod of whales. They would come up to the canoe, circle us, then swim off in a diagonal direction from the canoe. Then they did it again, and again, around the canoe, then off to the side diagonally from the canoe, where they would just kind of stay, watching us, then swim around us again.

Our captain, Bruce Blankenfeld, noticed a break in the clouds. One star shined bright. But with only one star, you cannot determine which direction to sail.

Then, Bruce looks at the whales and says, "Hey, the kohola, the whale, is the aumakua (*spiritual guardian*) for the canoe." We all nodded, and thought, "That's cool." We didn't give it any more thought at the time.

After awhile, the cloud cover started breaking up, there were some clear patches of sky and the wind picked up. Bruce could finally see enough stars to chart our course. After he turned the canoe in the direction we wanted to go, we noticed the whales were right in front of us. The whales had been pointing us in the direction we had wanted to go for days! We hadn't realized it because the stars — our normal navigational guidance — had been hidden.

Bruce says, "Brah, you're not going to believe this. The whales were telling us where to go."

That was unreal.

Then the sky cleared up and we headed straight for the Marquesas.

Like the First Man in the Moon

Early scientific theories were that voyagers sailed from the Americas to Polynesia carried by the wind and ocean currents. Hokulea was built, in part, to demonstrate that it was possible for Polynesians to sail against the wind, making a criss-cross pattern as they tacked into the wind as sailors do today. Dennis teaches his Hawaiian Studies students what he has learned sailing aboard Hokulea.

Getting to Hawaii from Polynesia is not unthinkable. As the ancient Polynesians began exploring, they learned techniques that allowed them to gradually sail out of sight of land. The limit, really, was how much food and water they could carry.

In going upwind, you're zig-zagging, and that expands your search area. You're covering more ground. If you don't find anything, then going back to your home is just a straight line downwind. Next time you could go off to an angle a little from where you went before, explore more and find a different island.

When Polynesians came to Hawaii, the first settlers probably came from the Marquesas Islands, then the second wave came from Tahiti. Some stories talk about expeditions in honor of alii (*royalty*), led by the king's second-in-command or maybe a younger brother.

A lot of it was and is the sense of adventure, that sense of wanting to go out there and find something. It was a way to build your own mana (*power*), to strike out and find your fortune. The canoe was like a spaceship: I founded an island! Who wants to be living under me? It was like being the first man on the moon.

It's Down to Honesty

My favorite part of sailing on canoes is being out with the rest of the guys, the camaraderie. You create such good ties with everyone you sail with. When you're on the ocean, you learn everybody's strengths and weaknesses. It's down to honesty. There are no pretenses. What you see is what you get, and you support each other however you can.

When voyages are over, it feels weird coming back to society. Some things are great, like hot water showers. But you miss the rest of your crew and the simplicity of it all. You try to hold the feeling you had on the canoe for as long as possible. When you return to daily life, at first you kind of ignore it for awhile, then you slowly get caught up in it again.

An anthropologist once told me that societies that come from canoes are formed based upon the values they learn while on the ca-noes, the values of kokua (*cooperation*), aloha (*compassion, kindness, awareness*), laulima (*working together*), respecting, understanding finite resources.

As a friend says, "When you're on the canoe, think island. When you're on the island, think canoe," in how you manage, how you live, the values that you create. We're all working together.

Taking Canoe Food To A New Level

Nalani Kaneakua

Nalani Kaneakua is a chef whose specialty is making everything from scratch using all fresh ingredients. After sailing on a number of training runs between the islands, she was selected to sail on Hokulea from Rapa Nui (Easter Island) to Tahiti in the fall of 1999, a 29-day journey, almost entirely on the open ocean. Speaking with her customary boundless energy and positivity, Nalani, born and raised in Anahola on Kauai, tells stories of sailing in Polynesian waters as the chef and only woman aboard this leg of Hokulea's world travels.

My dad was a commercial fisherman so I'd been out on big boats a lot fishing, sometimes for a few days, so I had my sea legs long before I was on Hokulea. It was second nature for me. On Hokulea, I'd be bouncing up and down and jumping all over and climbing here and hanging out there. On our voyage from Rapa Nui to Tahiti, I was the only female in the group of 13. A lot of the men didn't have their sea legs. Our doctor didn't have his sea legs for three weeks. We'd just send in crackers and tea for him.

On the canoe you have only a small space for yourself. Our compartments are in both of the hulls. They're so close together, someone else's foot is right behind your head, and your feet are right behind the next person's head, four or five people in each hull. There's a canvas flap over you so the water doesn't come in but it's not really sealed good so you get a little splashed. If the seas are calm, your sleep is calm. If they're big, you're getting thrashed around, water's flying up. For your personal belongings, you get two large dry bags and you stuff in whatever you can fit in there. I got a sleeping bag that's super, super thin but keeps you super, super warm.

I got selected to go on a long Hokulea journey because of my cooking skills. When we were doing some training on Oahu at different ports, swimming, running, getting dropped off in the ocean, getting thrown off, learning how to do the sails and the ropes, I got a call asking me to be the chef and quartermaster, in charge of supplies and provisions.

My kitchen on Hokulea was about two feet by three feet. I had a double propane burner. I had a bucket about 1½ feet tall to sit on; they padded it just for me. I had cutting boards and knives. There are other areas where we keep provisions like batteries and we can chop things on the top of those areas. Sometimes things happen fast, like the wind changes, so you can't leave anything lying around. You have to clean up fast.

I've always had a passion for nutrition, so I took what they normally put on board, just canned, powdered stuff, dried this and dried that, and incorporated a lot more healthy products. I introduced soy milk and rice milk. They loved it. The old timers still kind of had their stash of salty saimin (*noodle soup*). After maybe two weeks of eating my cooking, some of the old timers asked, "Could we just get a can of Spam?" I said "No!"

When we left Rapa Nui we were given fresh ginger, garlic, lemons, onions, herbs, basic spices and I had olive oil. We had eggs and all kinds of things we had to use before they went bad. The first night out, we left Rapa Nui in late afternoon. I made a big frittata, a big Italian omelet. The guys were really stoked. Then they wanted a frittata every morning. It was hilarious.

We were so blessed to have fish every day. I did everything I could think of with fish: I made sashimi, I made poke (*raw fish salad*), I made ceviche, poisson cru (*Tahitian fish salad*), soup. We used up every single part of the fish. We caught so much fish, we ran lines of dried fish. The whole boat was dried fish! I'd take them down and make a spicy dried poke.

They said they never gain weight on Hokulea sails, but I guess on my leg, everybody gained weight. They ate good every night. We had a lot of fresh produce for about the first two weeks. As it started going bad, I started to pickle the cabbage, pickle the turnips. We didn't touch our canned provisions for probably 20-some days then they were jonesing for Spam, so I made pancakes and put Spam in them. I made homemade tortillas. I made puto, a Filipino-style steamed muffin. When we were in Rapa Nui, I got a quick recipe for empanadas so I made empanadas with canned turkey. We had pumpkins, sweet potatoes and dried vegetables that we rehydrated.

One of my cooking qualities is my creativity and making everything from scratch so I was able to make unbelievable meals out of what we had. For instance, on Thanksgiving, I took some crackers, some boxed tofu and chocolate bars that I melted out on the deck. I made a crust with the crackers. I incorporated the chocolate with some honey into the tofu and mashed it, put it in the crust and put it up on the deck where it cooled in the night. We had chocolate tofu pie. Everyone's like, "Oh my God!" I took canoe food to a new level.

The other chefs or cooks on voyages after my leg, knew what I did, so it made them want to cook better. My friend Keala Kai told me, "Damn, Nalani, everybody talks about your food." Keala did really well. He's a really good cook, too.

We had three different watches. I cooked for each watch. I was up at 6 a.m. I did the morning breakfast as part of our watch. I prepared lunch, then I could relax, write in a journal or sleep. Then I prepared dinner. From 11 p.m. to 6 a.m. I could relax again. All the guys on my watch were right there to pass me this, wash that, pick up that. They'd say, "I'm Nalani's sous chef." They loved it. They all learned a lot, too.

It Gets Pretty Gnarly

Being out at sea for weeks, not seeing land, it's kind of scary. You come across some funky looking vessels and you wonder about them. Some of them would call us on the radio and ask, "Who are you guys?" We'd pass longliners, fishing longlines that go for miles. Some of the ships would try to get up close to us. A lot of them are working ships, they're moving cargo, so they couldn't stop and check us out.

We encountered a lot of orcas. The aumakua (*spiritual guardian*) for Hokulea is the whale. One overcast, cold night after the first week, everybody was still trying to get grounded. All of sudden about a half dozen orcas showed up and escorted us for a few hours on the left hand side of the canoe, almost until the sun came up. They were so darn close, you could see their eyes. We always had dolphins following us. We also had a pod of ahi tuna that stuck with us for the longest time. We caught an 80-pounder.

Sometimes I'd help steer, depending on the weather. When the seas are rough, everybody has to come on board. When the seas are really big, you have to run three steering sweeps. The sweeps are large wooden paddles about 24 feet long. Sometimes they tie you to a sweep in huge waves, three or four guys just hang on, you put your body weight on it. It gets pretty gnarly sometimes.

One night, one of our captains fell overboard. He went up to fix the mast and somehow he got tangled. He knew he was getting in trouble. He kept saying, "I think I'm going to fall." As he was falling, he hit his side on one of the hulls at the front of the boat. It was so dark. Everybody was right there but the canoe cannot stop. By the time you drop the sails, you're about one or two football fields away. The person who sees him fall yells, "Man Overboard!" That person has to point and keep an eye on him. A person in the back took the man overboard floater, clicked on the top light and threw it in the water and hollered, "The floater's in the water!" By the time the length of the boat went by, the captain came right up to the floating device. He got it and yelled, "I'm OK! I'm OK!" He clicked on the second light on the floater so our escort boat could see him and brought him in. That was two days before Thanksgiving.

Auntie, Let Me Use Your Powder

As the only woman aboard, the guys would tease me, just in fun. They'd ask, "Auntie, would you rub my shoulders?" I'd say, "No, I don't do that. I don't give massages. I don't wash clothes." They'd tease me more. I'd tell them "No!" They'd joke back, "Oh, Auntie, you junk!"

They respected my space. They set up a way for me to take my bath with a privacy canvas, and the escort boat was far enough behind they didn't see anything. You go out at the very end of the boat and put a harness on. The canoe doesn't stop for anybody. You pour water over your head with a small bucket and use soap and special shampoo that washes off the salt water. When I'd go take a bath, the guys would throw things over the privacy barrier!

After I was done, I'd go into my compartment, powder up and get all nice and warm. The guys would say, "Auntie, let me use your powder." It was fun.

Life Altering

Being on the canoe was life altering. I would go again in a heartbeat. On the canoe, I wasn't Mom. I was Nalani.

When you get home, you do a lot of soul searching, thinking about where you've been and where you want to go. When I came back I totally appreciated everything around me. On the canoe, you only had what you had. For me, having nothing was very freeing. Having each other, that's more important than having all these fine things. I don't really desire a lot, so it was easy for me to be on the canoe, but it reaffirmed my belief about being simple. I feel you can have a lot and do a lot with nothing.

It was so meaningful to be out there on the canoe, because it was like survival. We needed to move together, to work together to make the canoe move. It's the same here on the island. In order to make things work, we need to work together. We pull together as a team, our kids and our family. It doesn't take much to be happy as long as we have each other.

Nalani Kaneakua
(Photo by Ron Kosen — Photo Spectrum)

It's Magic
Keala Kai

Keala Kai, a strong and gentle Hawaiian man, speaks poetically of his experiences sailing Polynesian-style and the connection he made with his ancestors while aboard Hokulea. A former professional lifeguard who was born and raised on Kauai, Keala was invited on his first Hokulea voyage in 2005 when he was 47 years old. Since then, he has sailed on Hokulea from Fukuoka, Japan to Oshima and then onto Uwajima; and from Hawaii to Palmyra Atoll in the central Pacific. After returning from his voyages, Keala was inspired to launch a new career as an artist, drawing intricate pencil sketches of sailing canoes of all shapes and sizes on canvasses and for his own line of clothing.

Sailing Among the Stars

The first thing that kind of grabs you is the sound a voyaging canoe makes when it's just sitting. All the tension of the cords and the sails, it's almost like the canoe is alive and it wants to go somewhere.

Before I ever sailed on Hokulea, I was sitting on a box on the canoe one day when she was moored at Nawiliwili Harbor on Kauai. Dennis Chun and other people that I read about in school, were discussing a sailing plan to Oahu. If I had just had that one moment, that would have been enough for me, just to be on the canoe with these people. Then out of the blue, Dennis and John Kruse *(the first*

Kauai resident to sail on Hokulea), turned around at the same time and said, "Hey, Keala, what you doing tomorrow? You want to go sailing with us?" I had a lump in my throat and couldn't answer. I just nodded.

My great-grandmother could speak Hawaiian but I can't. But the next morning before we left, when we formed a circle on the canoe and the prayer was said in Hawaiian, it's almost like some kind of ancestral knowledge came over me and I understood exactly what they were saying, even though I didn't know the words. I could feel it. It was electric.

Then we went sailing.

Someone told me, "When you're out there, the stars come down so low, it's like Hokulea is lifting you up into the heavens, and you're sailing among the stars." Whenever you go aboard the Hokulea, it's magic.

Nobody Said a Word

My first crossing of the channel between Kauai and Oahu was on the eve of my great-grandmother's birthday. The ocean was very rough that night. Just a little after midnight, I was given the opportunity to take over the steering on the sweep. The sweep is a large wooden paddle that's 24 feet and 10 inches long. They told me to follow a particular star. But you're steering this canoe that's like 20,000 pounds and there are so many things that are happening at the same time: the wind direction, the waves, the drift, the hydraulics aboard the canoe, the weight of the sail.

Suddenly, the wind died down and I couldn't feel which direction it was coming from. There's a thing called the "no-sail" zone. You go in there and you can't sail out because there's no wind. And I got us in there. Everybody was sleeping except me and about three other people, but they all knew what was happening by the sound of the sail. I heard all the zippers of their compartments unzip as the whole crew woke up and came on deck. They started to une (*paddle*) to turn the canoe around. It took about 25 minutes. Nobody said a word.

Finally they gave the steering back to me. Dennis said, "Now, don't do that again." About an hour later, I did it one more time. They all came up again and they all helped me une it again. I felt so bad, but there's no place you can hide. The whole working space on the canoe is only about 10 feet by 40 feet.

After we got going again, John was on the sweep and he said, "Hey, where's Keala?" I didn't want to answer. He said, "Get back on this sweep." He handed it over to me. He said, "One day I'll tell you the story about how all the great navigators spun this canoe around. You think you're the only one who did this? They all did. But that's how you learn."

I started drawing canoes while I was on this voyage. When John needed something built on Hokulea, he'd explain it to me. If I didn't quite understand, I'd put it to picture and draw the components. John would say, "Yeah, just like that!" It took off from there. Whenever I had to make something for the canoe, I would draw it.

When I started to draw my own canoes, it was very easy for me because I had already drawn all the individual parts.

My grandfather taught me, "If you can draw something, you can build it." And that's what happened. I had the best teacher in the world: Hokulea.

Thousands of Ancestors Step With You

Before we left Hawaii for the 1,000-mile sail to Palmyra, Nainoa Thompson, our top navigator, gave a speech to the crew. He told us,

"When you step on that canoe, thousands of Hawaiians step with you. And when you step off that canoe, thousands of ancestors step with you, too. Never forget that."

It reminded me of when I was a young kid, we had a small taro patch on our property in Haena. My grandfather's brother, my uncle, used to ask me to help him clean taro. One day, I must have been about 10, I saw our reflection in the water. I said, "Look at us. It's pretty cool." He looked at me and said, "That's not you. That's not me. That's all your ancestors looking back at you. Whenever you feel alone, you look in the water and they're there. It took a thousand years of them to make you." I was a little kid; I didn't understand it.

Before we left for Palmyra Atoll, I flew from Kauai to Oahu where Hokulea was moored. A storm came up and we had to delay our departure. I slept aboard the canoe for 13 nights until the storm passed and it was safe for us to leave. On one of those nights, I'm sitting on the pier, playing my guitar, I look in the water and I see my reflection. Then it came back to me, what my uncle told me 40 years ago, and what Nainoa said about our representing the Hawaiian people. I started to transform myself into what was needed to perform that task.

When you're sailing, the farther you go out into the middle of the ocean, you become more in tune with the ancestors who came from Polynesia. They had it rough. Their canoes sat much lower in the water, and they didn't have foul weather gear. They didn't have Cup of Noodle soup. You realize how hard it must have been for them. You get more connected with your ancestry, because now you appreciate how brave these people were to come that far.

You start hearing voices, not with your ears, but with your heart, because you're in a different realm. You understand the theory of malama, take care of one another, because that's the only way your canoe is going to be safe out there.

Hawaiian Culture Stands For Peace

Hokulea takes you to extraordinary places, you meet extraordinary people and you have extraordinary experiences. It's like the stuff in your wildest dreams.

When we were going from Fukuoka to Suoshima, Japan in 2007, the Japanese people wanted us to stop at Uwajima island to give us something. When we got there, there were about 10 huge fishing boats with huge flags. Out comes a big rowboat with about 20 priests in it and somebody in the middle holding a lantern that held the fire of Hiroshima from the atomic blast in 1945.

The story they told us is that after the U.S. dropped the nuclear bomb, a woman was worried about her brother who lived in Hiroshima. She sent her grandson to find him. When the grandson got to the bookstore where the brother had been, it was gone, flattened. The grandson went down into the basement, took some embers, put them in a hand warmer and brought them back to his grandmother where the embers became a flame. It was a hate flame. The grandmother kept the embers and prayed every day to the flame and it became a healing flame.

When the 1964 Olympics were held in Japan, they used that flame to light the Olympic flame. When they made the Atomic Dome museum in Hiroshima, the two stainless steel hands at the entrance hold an eternal flame that was lit from the same woman's lantern. She kept that flame going for more than 60 years.

The priests on the rowboat in Japan gave the woman's lantern to us. They told us it was time for the generations to move forward in peace. They said the Hokulea and the Hawaiian culture stand for peace and compassion, so they wanted us to take the lantern and extinguish the flame.

Our captain said, "I don't care what you guys do, just make sure that that fire does not go out." We didn't know where to put it. Everybody was scared to hold it. We put it in a box and we stood around that box, just making sure that light didn't go out.

When we got to Suoshima, lots of people were up on the docks looking down at us. They knew we had the lantern. We came onto the deck of Hokulea, then onto the pier. We looked up at all the people and said, "Let's extinguish this flame here."

When they gave us that flame, they also had given us a package that held a stick and small candle. The flame represented the older generation and the small candle represented the future generation. They told us to light the stick with the lantern flame, say a prayer, then with the stick, light the small candle, which represented the future generation, and say a prayer to move forward. We, the crew, all got down on our knees and formed a circle. We said the prayers and said a prayer in Hawaiian, too. Then our crew member, Attwood Makanani, took sea water held in a coconut shell to represent the water of the whole world, and poured it on the small candle to extinguish it. Our captain gave Nainoa Thompson the privilege of lowering the light in the lantern until it went out forever.

When we blew out that flame, we knew we did something of great significance but it didn't sink in because it's like you don't believe what you just did, what you just saw, what you just witnessed. Nobody said a word. Somebody started moving back to Hokulea. I guess because we're from Hokulea, we felt safe on her. Spontaneously, we broke into the haka *(a traditional New Zealand tribal dance)* and the canoe was rocking. It was really emotional. The people up there saw it and they were making big noise. It was amazing.

The Stories Will Never End

Sailing on a voyaging canoe lifts you so high, it gives you a window so you can see your ancestors. All the people you sail with, they lift you on their shoulders so you can look through that window. When you're around people like that, they let you dare to dream.

We just launched our own voyaging canoe for Kauai, the Namahoe, for the next generation to get on a canoe and go somewhere. It's 70 feet long and has twin hulls. Namahoe translated means "the twins," for her two hulls. It's also the Hawaiian name for the constellation Gemini, also the twins, the principal guiding stars between Oahu and Kauai during certain times of the year. Namahoe will provide more opportunities for Kauai people to experience the magic of sailing the way our ancestors did. Pick a star and go. Hey, why not?

Namahoe is a gift to all the people of Hawaii. That canoe embodies all the principles we need on a world stage: sustainability, taking care of natural resources, living together. What we're trying to create on the canoe, it's the same thing we're trying to create on this island.

I would love to bring someone onto a Polynesian voyaging canoe and tell them the same thing I was told. "Why don't you go sailing so you can make your own history, because I want to hear your story."

And the stories will never end.

Keala Kai with one of Hokulea's three steering sweeps while the boat is docked at Nawiliwili Harbor on Kauai. (Photo by Pamela Varma Brown)

www.KauaiStories.net